ABANDONED
LOS ANGELES

A COUNTY REDISCOVERED

KIMBERLY LANDMARK

AMERICA
—
THROUGH
—
TIME

America Through Time
www.through-time.com

First published 2025
Copyright © Kimberly Landmark 2025

ISBN 978-1-63499-501-6

Typeset in Trade Gothic 10pt on 15pt
Printed and bound in England

CONTENTS

INTRODUCTION

Growing up, my parents made certain that we lived a very active and adventurous lifestyle. Some of my earliest memories include road trips, camping, boating, and exploring countless destinations. Luckily, my dad always had a camera in his hand, so many of my memories are enhanced by pictures and he always stressed the importance of capturing moments on film so that I could look back on them forever. It was not long before I wanted to have a camera of my own, and so it began with a cheap used polaroid and an abundance of disposables. Once my parents realized that I was truly passionate about photography, they bought me my very own digital camera. Although it was just a small little pocket camera, I absolutely loved it. I was always adventuring with my family, and featured in their photographs, but now the pictures would be different. Now I was able to get creative, and capture memories from my point of view to create my own album to tell the stories of my experiences to anyone who looked through them. This idea really fascinated me, and I was excited to capture my next adventure on camera.

I believe that my love for urban exploring began when I was four years old, and my dad got a job as a ranch hand on a 200-acre ranch in Lake Hughes California. We had our own little two-bedroom house on the property, and we spent our days riding around on ATCs, chasing frogs, dancing in the clubhouse, and floating on the pond. I was very young, so many of my memories were created from photographs, home videos, and stories, but one memory that stands out the most is riding up to the remains of an old homestead on the property. Not much was left of it, but I still found it very fascinating and my interest in urban exploration blossomed quickly from there. What was once a fun hobby quickly turned into a passion, and I began to hunt these locations down on my own.

I decided that I wanted to learn and understand the history of photography and of my state, California, as well as what leads homes to neglect and abandonment. I began to realize how little I knew about the area I had been exploring for years. Some buildings have been restored so well that it is hard to recognize their true age, while others, which have stood gloriously for over 100 years, are decaying, pigeon infested, and falling to pieces. The reasoning behind what leads a home or building to its extreme state of neglect really varies, but often it is due to financial factors; yet when the structure is considered a historic landmark, there are strict laws that prevent any demolition from taking place. So, there they remain, slowly deteriorating, and patiently waiting to be loved again.

If walls could talk, what stories would they choose to share, and which would they sweep under the rug? We may never know exactly what happened inside these mysterious structures, but luckily, we do have some historical records, family folklore, vivid imaginations, and, if we are lucky, photographs. Regardless, if there are solid facts or just theories, I believe each building has an interesting story, worthy of exploring and sharing, even those falling apart to the elements of neglect. With caution, I want to take you on a journey through the eclectic past of several of Los Angeles County's most notorious abandoned places, going through the destruction to rediscover the beauty and stories that lie within the dilapidated walls. We will cover the beautiful county of Los Angeles, focusing on some of the darkest and most mysterious places in the area. Travel from the heart of Downtown Los Angeles to the beautiful mountain ranges of Santa Monica, the high desert to old gold and oil mines and eerily abandoned mansions. From one spooky place to another, there are many neglected sites waiting to be discovered once again.

1

LOST IN LOS ANGELES

Los Angeles is home to about 9.8 million people, and throughout history, it has homed some of the most influential artists, architects, and designers in the world. The county was officially established at the time of statehood in 1850, and it was of the very first counties in all of California. Since then, a lot has changed, and many historic structures have either been knocked down to build new developments or have been restored and preserved; very few sit abandoned with no future in site. New laws protect historic buildings from being demolished, but simultaneously the city does not have the funds to restore them all. Many crumble while they wait, patiently and vacant, hoping to be restored, while others have been left in shambles, as a reminder of Los Angeles's vast historical background.

Old L.A. Zoo

To kick off the journey, I would like to start with one of Los Angeles's most notorious abandoned locations, the Old L.A. Zoo at Griffith Park. What started as one man's dream to construct the world's greatest zoo became a small, low-budget version of what he had imagined. In 1912, the L.A. City Council funded the construction of the zoo with a lot less money than the designers had envisioned, which led to many architectural corners being cut.

Approximately fifteen animals populated the zoo when the establishment first opened, but by 1913 that number had grown to nearly 100, many of which were rescued. By the 1950s, the animal population had grown to over 1,000 despite structural flaws, and the zoo became known for having overcrowded quarters, small animals escaping, and animals obtaining significant injuries. Inevitably, the zoo began to develop an unbelievably bad reputation and the complaints continued to pour in, but it was not until 1966 that the zoo officially closed its doors for good. It has since become a haven for explorers, and although many structures have been removed, most of the cages and bear pits are still found in the park to this day.[1]

This zoo once attracted people from all over Los Angeles County, and it held many diverse types of animals, including bears, wolves, monkeys, cougars, exotic birds, wild cats, and more. As I walk these empty paths, lined with rusted cages, I imagine how the first guest must have felt seeing wild animals in person for the first time ever.

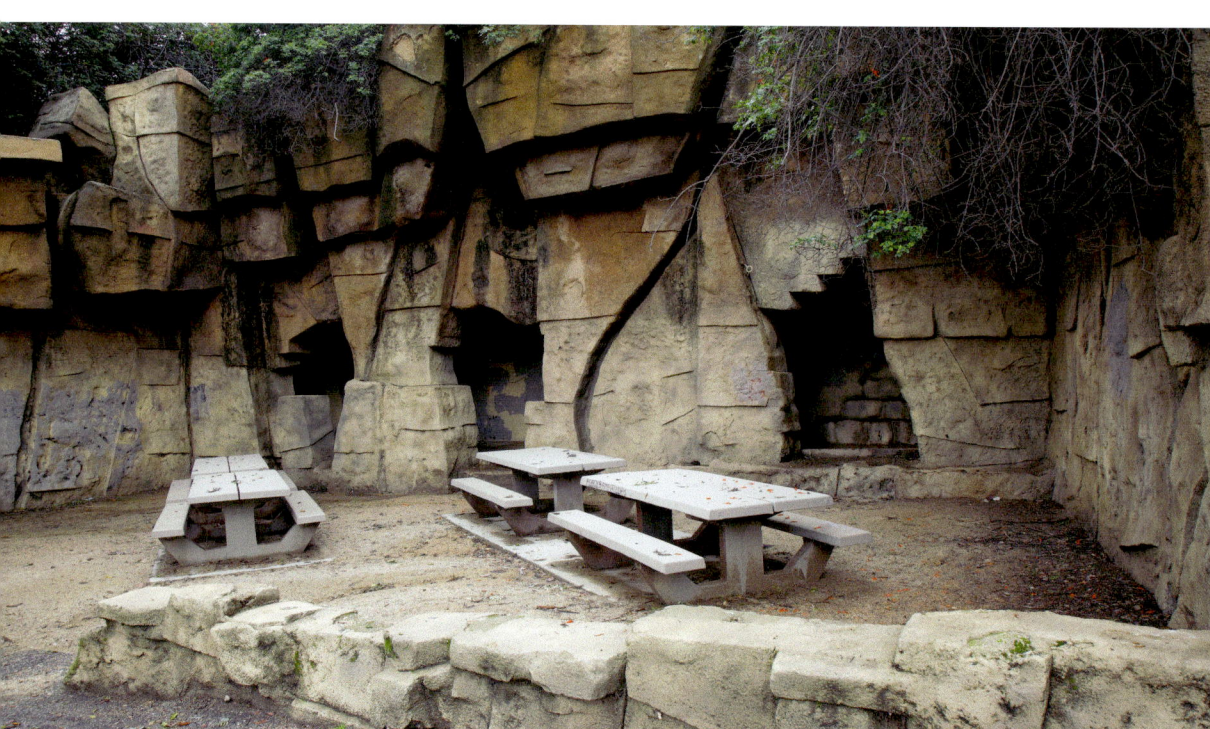

These man-made rock grottos, which once held polar bears and lions, now hold picnic tables where curious spectators can enjoy their lunch while immersed in the ruins of the Old L.A. Zoo.

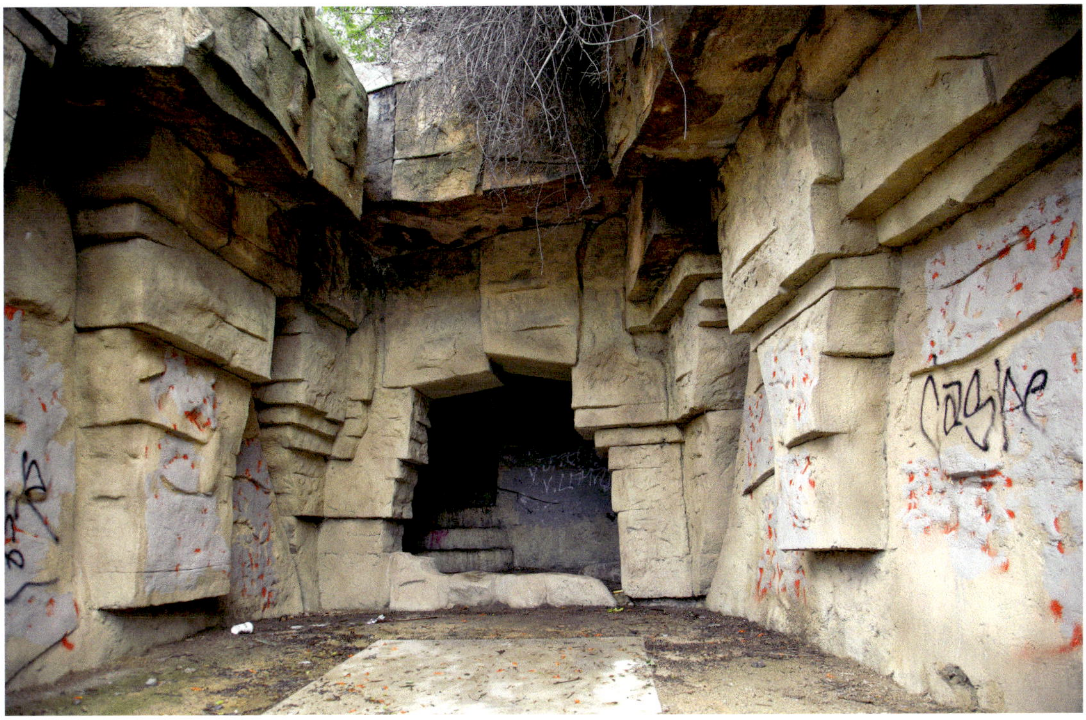

This grotto was one of the last structures built at the zoo before its closure in 1966.

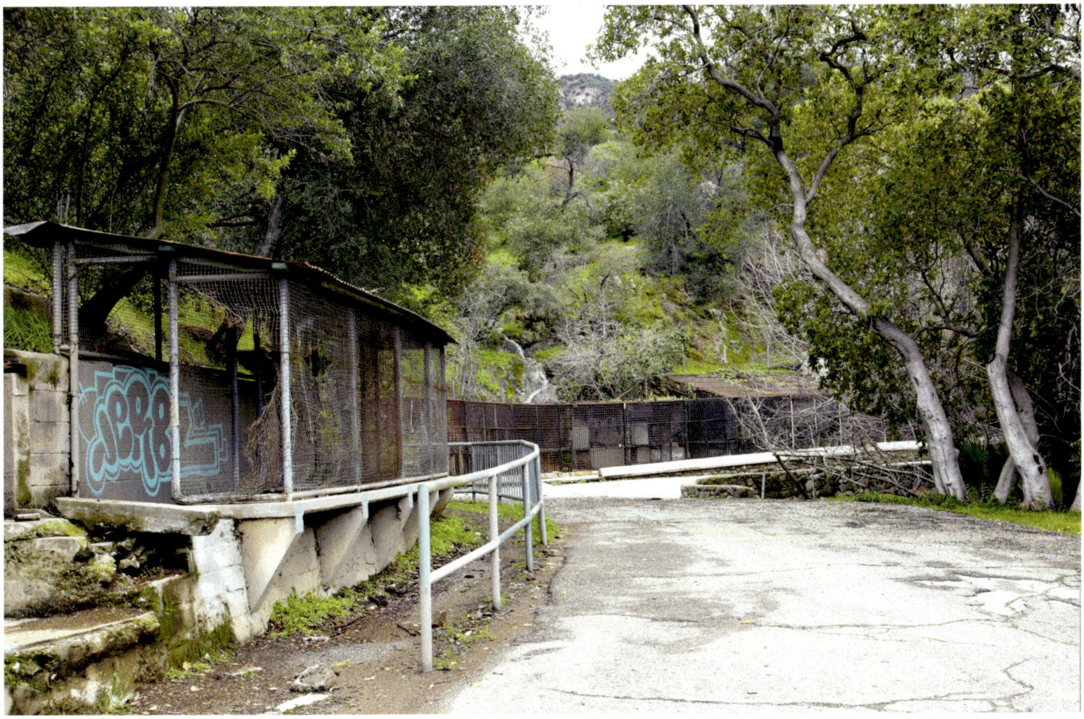

Walking these paths and observing these enclosures, it is very saddening to imagine large wild animals cooped up in these small cages.

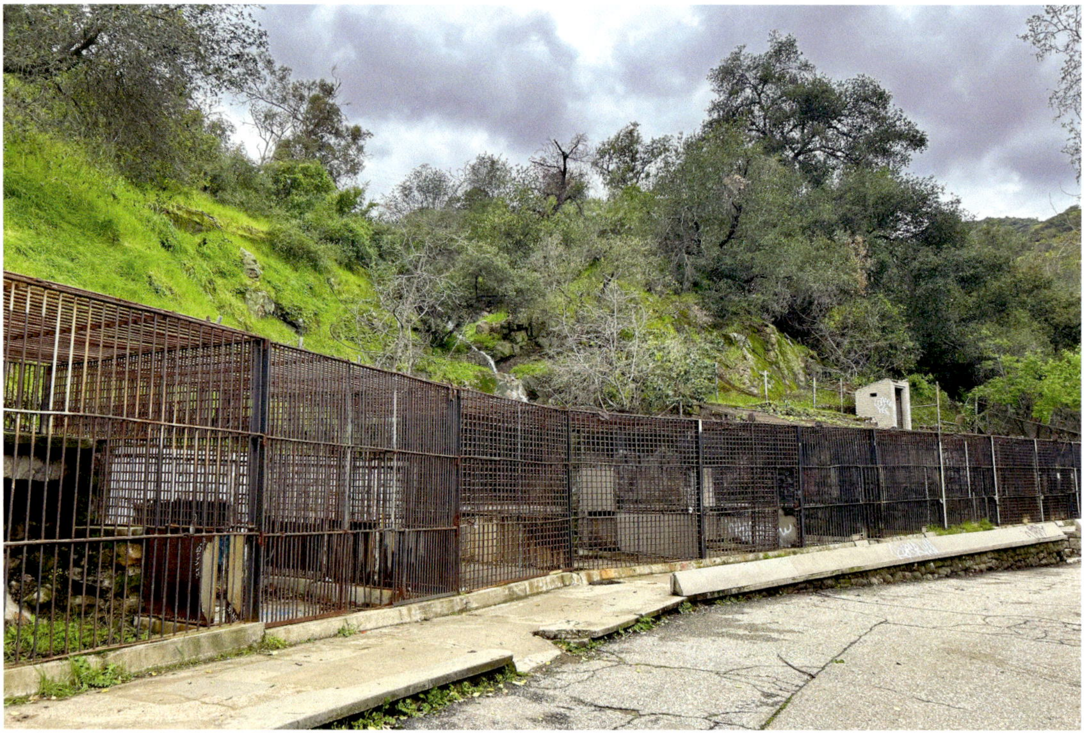

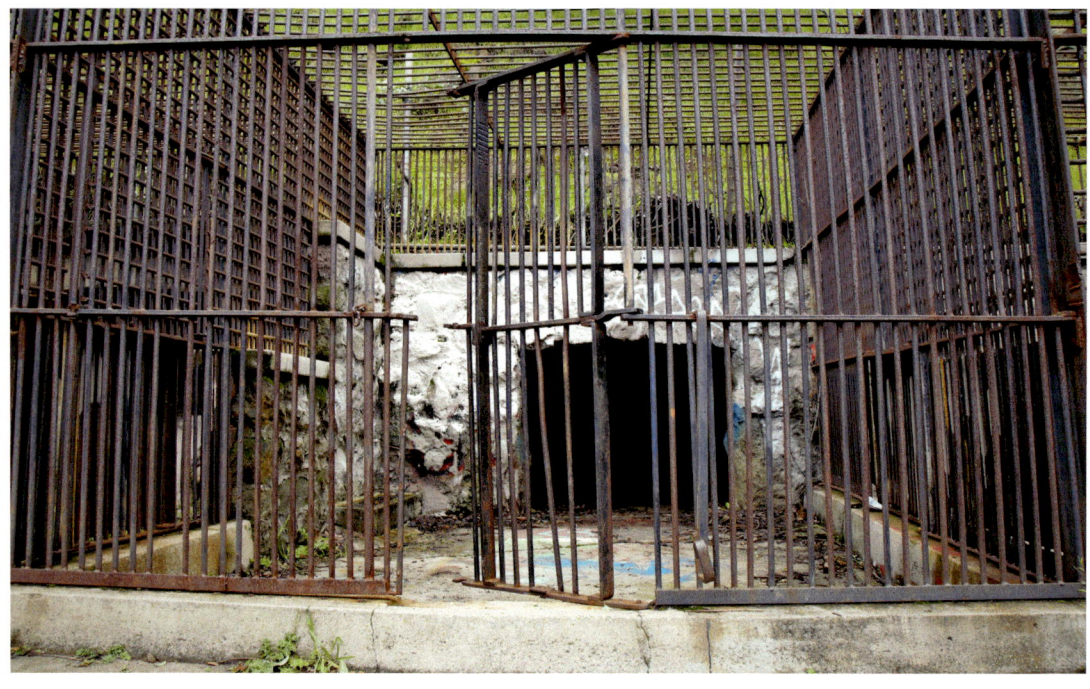

When heavy rain hits Los Angeles, a small waterfall begins to form behind the cages. Back in the '50s, the old zoo would often flood, which led to several animals escaping their enclosures.

On November 28, 1966, the cage doors were opened for the last time, and all animals were finally transferred to more suitable homes.

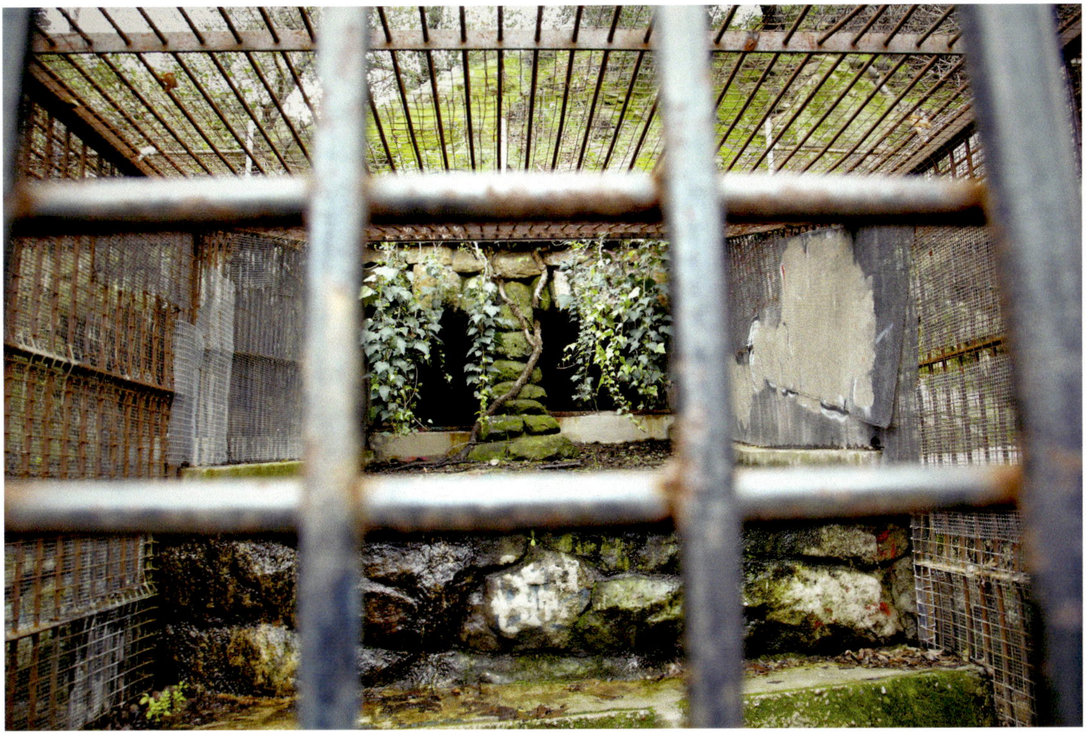

Above: All that remains in the cages are overgrown ivy, moss, and puddles, but some people believe that these cages are haunted by the poor animals that lost their lives due to the harsh conditions of the zoo.

Right: These pathways enclosed behind the grottos, consisting of steep staircases and narrow tunnels, were used for the staff to have easy access to care for the animals.

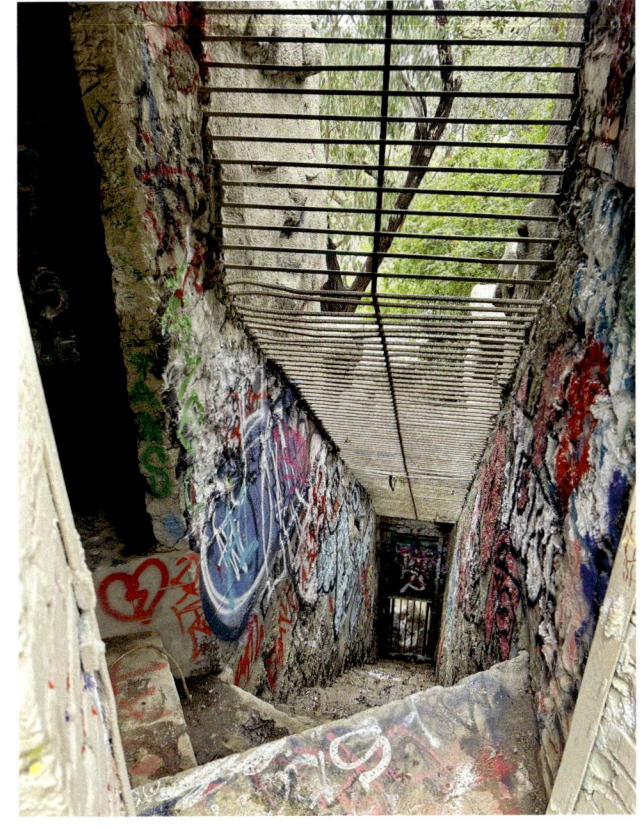

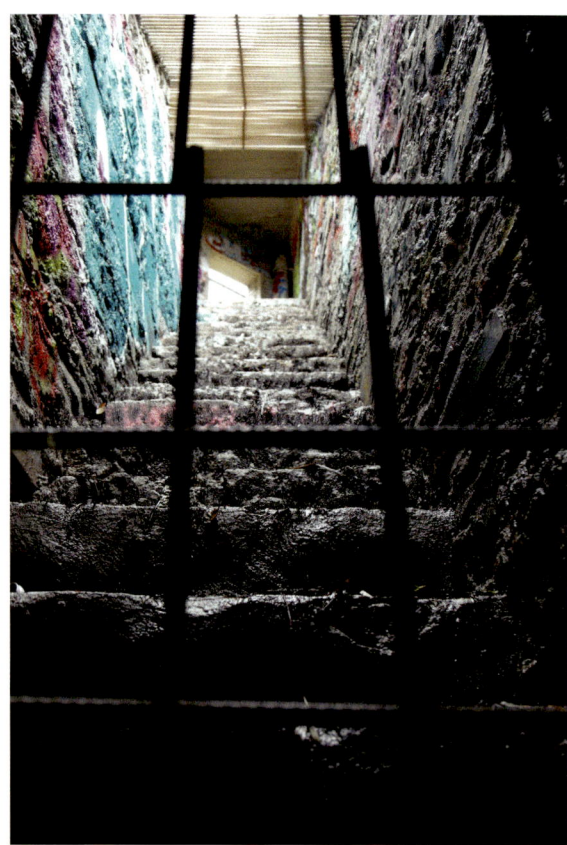

Left: This enclosure seems to also have been affected by flooding and is slowly filling up with sand from the hillside.

Below: Due to multiple injuries obtained by curious visitors, these paths are now blocked by steel bars to prevent anyone else from getting hurt.

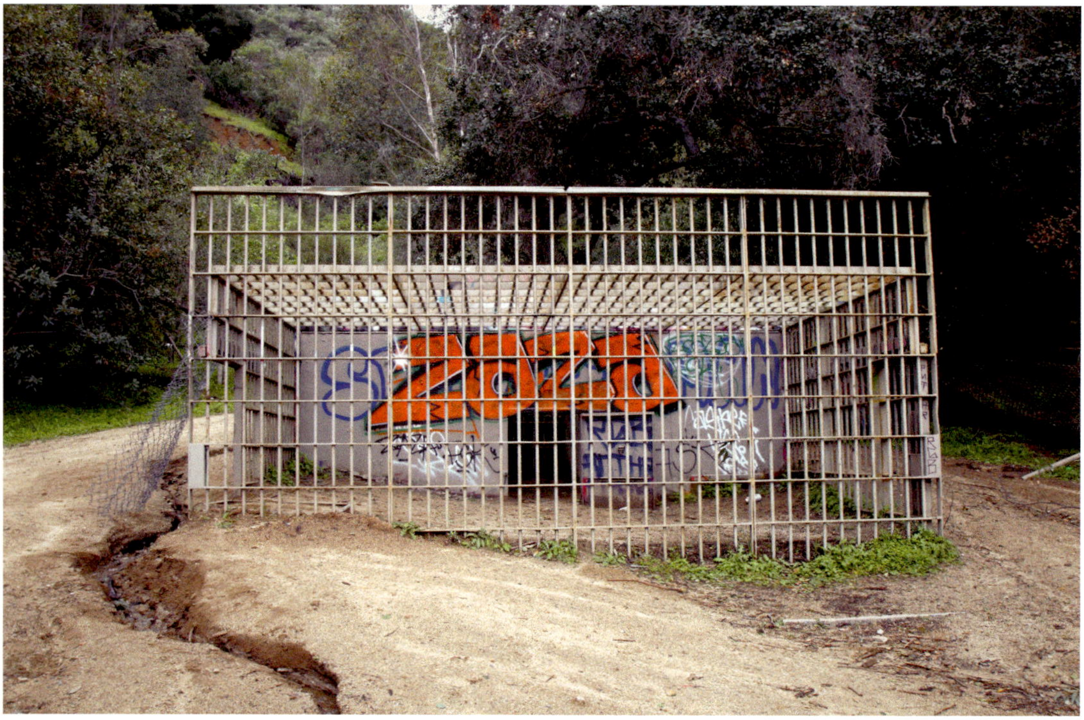

Barlow Sanitorium

Less than a half of a mile from the notorious Dodger Stadium sits the dilapidated bungalows of the historic Barlow Sanitorium, which was built in 1902 by physician Jarvis Barlow to care for tuberculosis patients. At the time, no drugs existed that could treat nor cure the disease, and it was killing Americans at an alarming rate. He decided to build the sanitorium because he believed that he was cured by traveling to the sunny, dry climate of California and he was convinced other patients would experience the same results.

When the facility first opened, he housed and cared for thirty-four patients with the help of a small team of nurses. Across from the main hospital was a row of cottages, which often housed multiple patients at one time. These close quarters often led to great friendships and a sense of community among the patients. Eventually, antibiotics were developed and the need for isolation and prolonged treatment decreased rapidly. This eventually led to the facility transforming and broadening its services to cover diagnosis and treatment of other chronic respiratory diseases.[2]

The entire treatment center is now registered as a historic landmark and has undergone extensive renovations over the past few decades. Always focusing on the main hospital and immediate surrounding buildings, the cottages have been neglected by the restoration team due to lack of funding. So, there they sit, as a significant reminder of a very dark, but eye-opening time in the history of L.A.

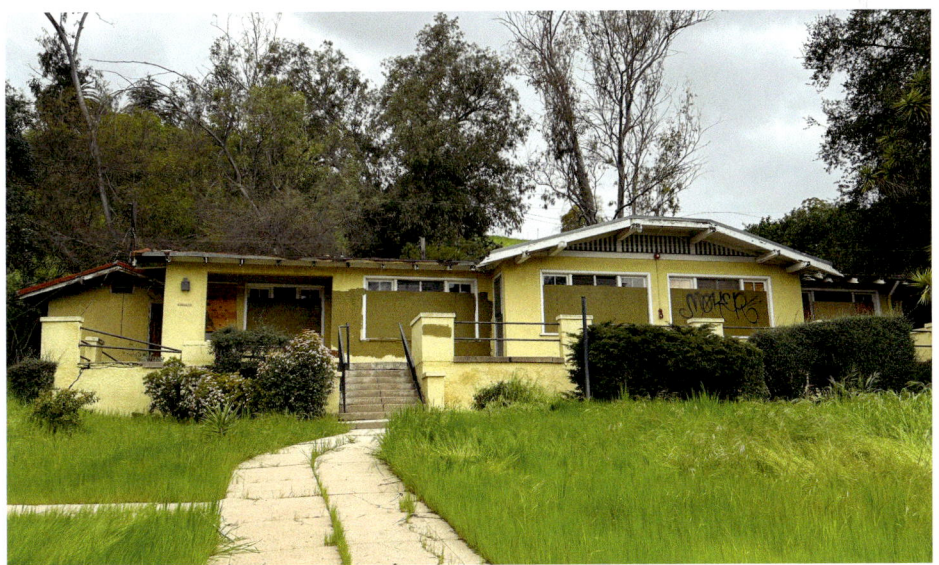

These bungalows once housed long-term tuberculosis patients, to give them a sense of a normal lifestyle while undergoing treatment in quarantine.

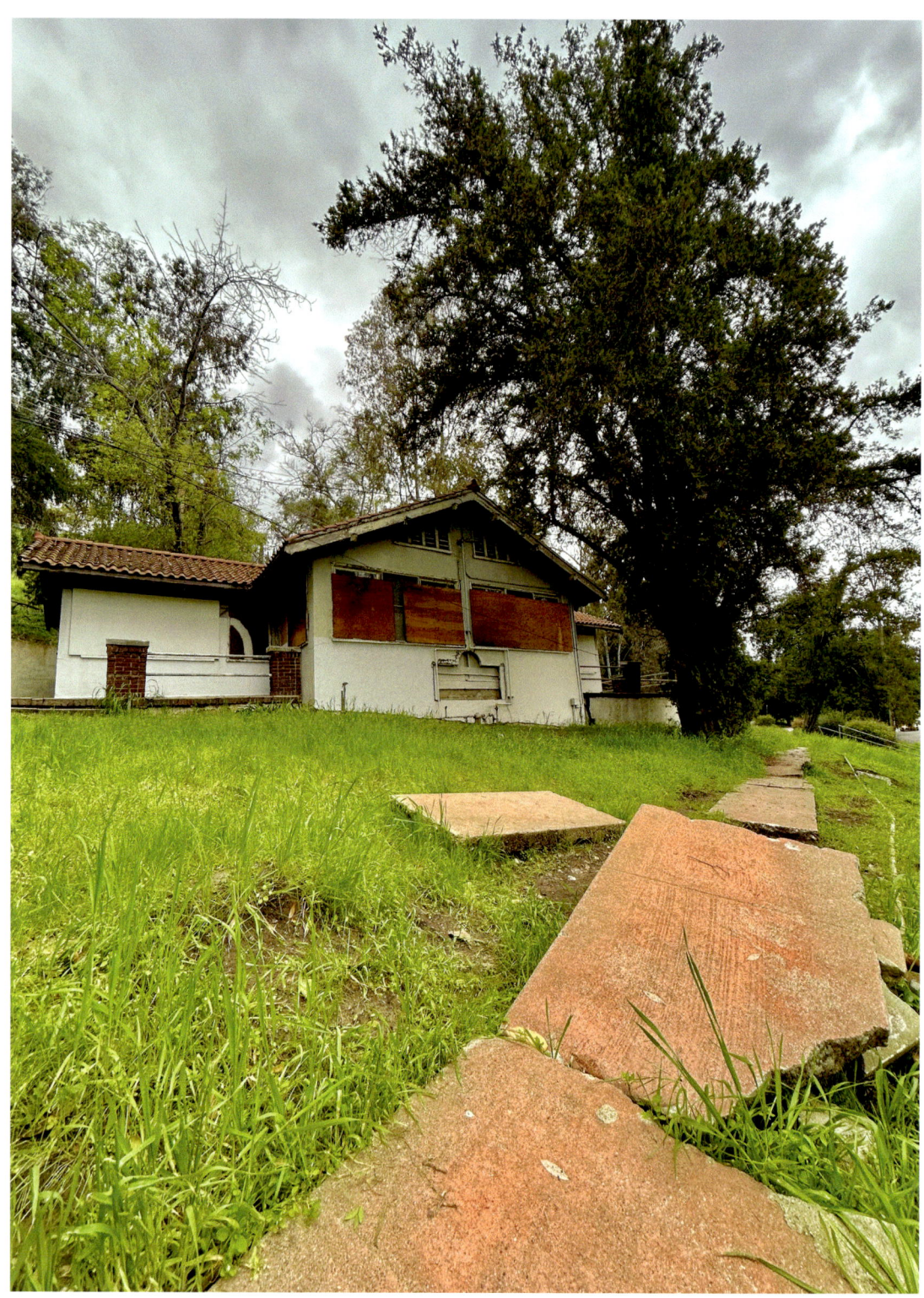

An unstable and treacherous pathway leads to the row of dilapidated bungalows along the hillside at Barlow Respiratory Hospital.

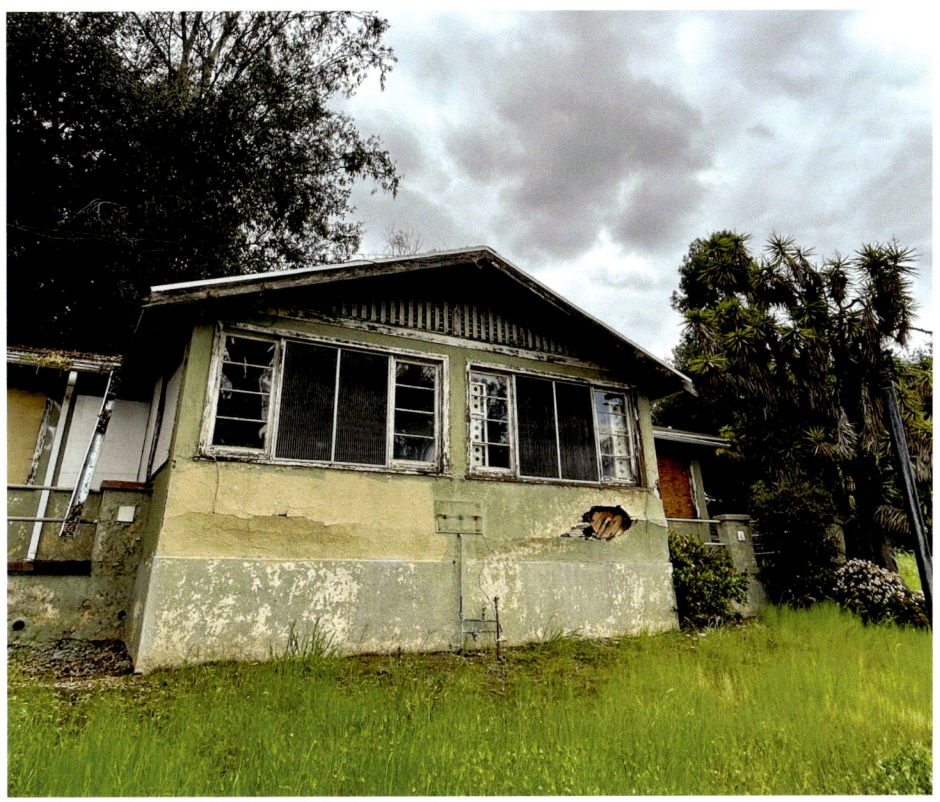

The bungalows seem to be preserved, but there is no sign of any restoration or future restoration plans taking place.

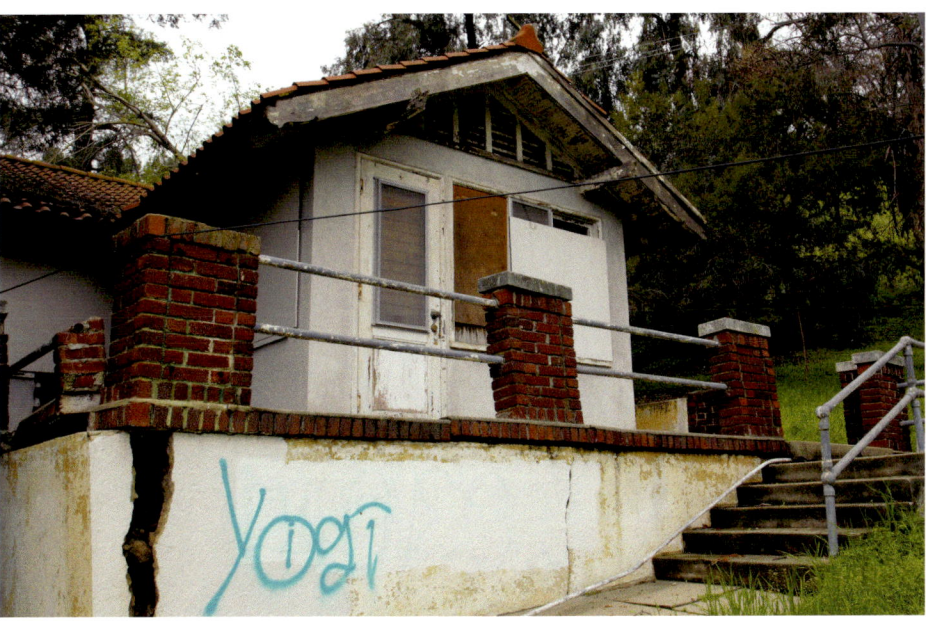

Although these cottages gave people a more normal lifestyle, the patients still had to abide by strict hospital policies, including no loud noises, lights out at 9 p.m., and a cold plunge every morning.

Lincoln Heights Jail

The historic Lincoln Heights Jail first opened its doors in 1931, as one of the largest jails in the area, capable of housing up to 625 inmates at full capacity. Unfortunately, the jail was notoriously overcrowded and at one time had an estimated 2,800 inmates crammed into its walls. That was until 1951 when the city finally approved an expansion to be added to accommodate up to 4,000 prisoners. It was a relief for both inmates and staff, but the jail had much larger internal issues than just population alone; the institution was full of corrupt officers and the abuse complaints were endless. The most notable event was on the evening of December 24, 1951, when a fight broke out between seven men and a group of LAPD officers over a call of a suspected group of underage boys drinking in public. When officers arrived on the scene, they realized the men were all of age, but they decided to forcefully try to remove the men anyway. A fight broke out, and although it was brief, it resulted in several officers with bloody noses, black eyes, and a deep desire for revenge. Six of the seven men were arrested and booked at Lincoln Heights Jail by the end of that night. Little did they know that rumors were developing quickly when several officers did not show up to the annual LAPD holiday party being held that evening. It is believed that one of the officers was exaggerating his recollection of the brawl that took place that day, and angrily led a group of furious officers to perform the gruesome attack on the inmates. This altercation would soon lead to one of L.A.'s first, and most famous, police brutality cases in its history. Referred to as "The Bloody Christmas," it was a day that brought awareness to the corruption going on inside of Lincoln Heights Jail. The six inmates were pulled from their cells and brutally beaten for over an hour and thirty minutes by a mob of fifty police officers.

The attack was so severe, and witnessed by so many, that it was nearly impossible for the department to cover up this incident, although they did try. The court case made history because it was the first case of police brutality to result in an indictment against an LAPD officer. They tried extremely hard to cover their tracks, and unfortunately only five officers were found guilty of their crimes, while forty-five others were transferred to other jails.[3] This did not end the corruption, but after a budget review, the city decided to decommission the jail for good and distribute the prisoners to other jails in L.A. County. The building was later used for the Bilingual Foundation of the Arts until it officially closed its doors for the last time in 2014.

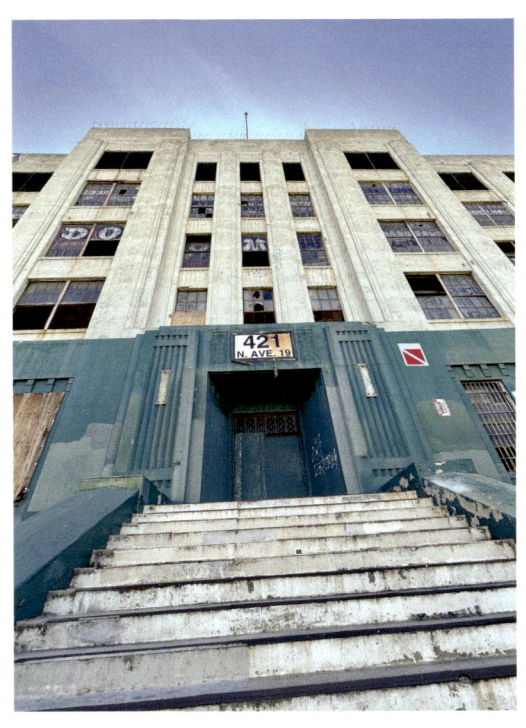

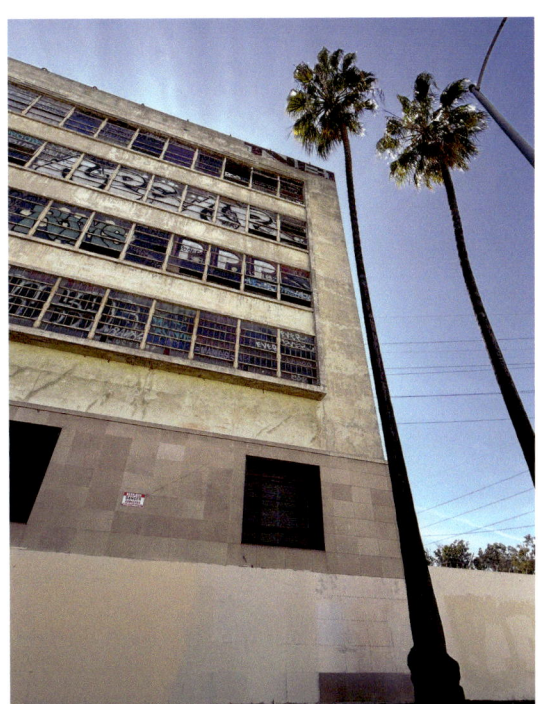

Above left: In 1927, the Lincoln Heights Jail construction began, with a budget of $5 million. American architects Jesse E. Stanton and Gordon B., with the help of a dedicated team of construction workers, erected a five-story Art Deco-style building.

Above right: These walls would later hold many notorious criminals, including Al Capone and actress Lucille Watson.

Right: Unfortunately, it also staffed many corrupt police officers and was the site of one of the most tragic police brutality cases in Los Angeles history—known as "The Bloody Christmas."

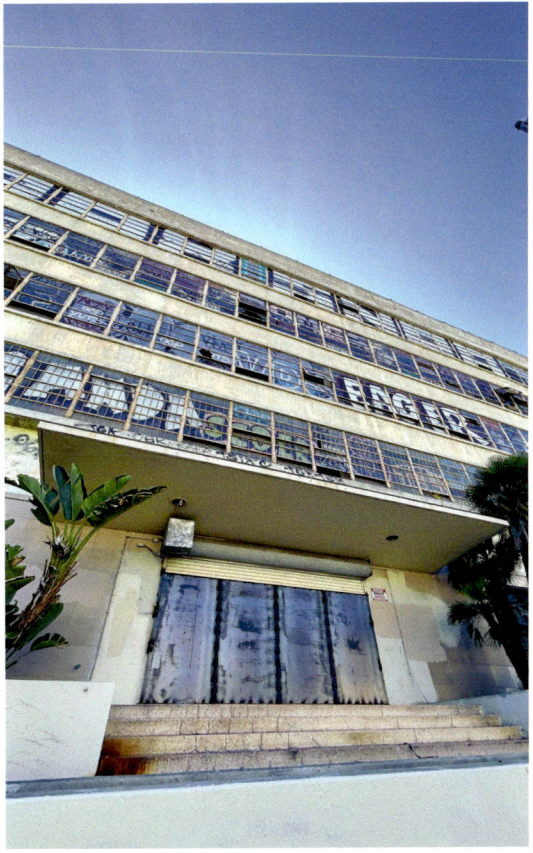

Garfield Building

The Garfield Building is known for its Art Deco design, unique floral reliefs, iron accents, and its boarded windows. It is always mind blowing to see abandoned buildings of such an enormous size sitting vacant for decades in a city where property value is so high. Built in 1929, it was originally a luxurious twelve-story office space; now, it is a registered historic landmark that has sat abandoned in the heart of Downtown Los Angeles for over thirty years. The building was sold in March 2022, and there are rumors that the new owners plan to convert it into a boutique hotel. It has been considered one of the worst eyesores in Los Angeles by those who do not see its potential, but hopefully the new investors can turn that image around and bring this beauty back to life.

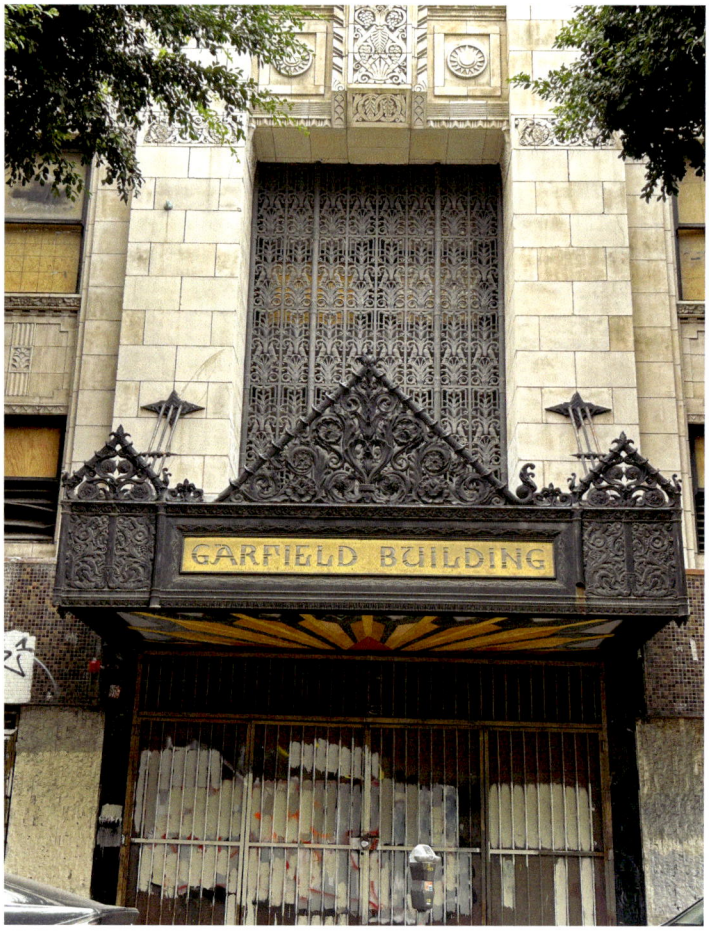

The Garfield building is a perfect example of Art Deco combined with a floral Art Nouveau style, which both were very popular during the time of its construction in the late 1920s.

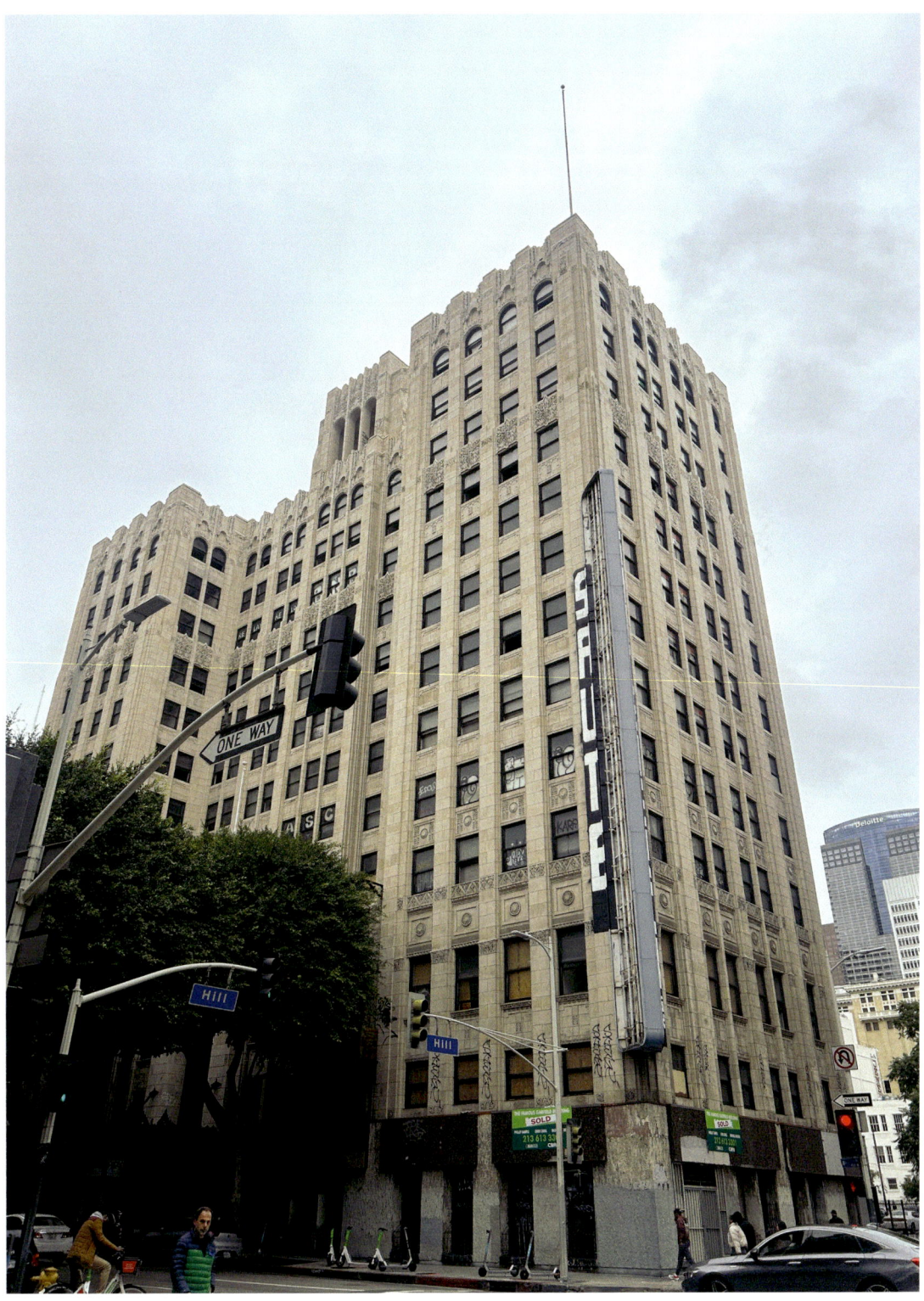

The Garfield building holds the title of one of L.A.'s worst eyesores, but it was recently sold to investors in March 2022 and locals hold tight to their hopes of this company renovating this historic Los Angeles landmark.

The L.A. County Poor Farm

The L.A. County Poor Farm, also known as the Rancho Los Amigos, has a very extensive and iconic history. It was founded and constructed in 1888 by the county of Los Angeles as a sanctuary for the elderly, disabled, mentally ill, and homeless; it was to house and employ people who were in need. The crops and livestock were maintained by the more healthy and active residents, while the less able had access to the care they needed. The property became highly successful and soon grew to house thousands of patients.[4] The property even had its own zoo, library, auditorium, rail lines, and, at one point, was even recognized as its own city before being incorporated into the city of Downey. The facade was short-lived, and the treatment center began to receive complaints about patient abuse and several patients even ended their own lives while under the supervision of this facility. In 1932, the Poor Farm was headed for change, starting with a change of name. Rancho Los Amigos, which translates to "The Ranch of the Friends," was a new beginning for the farm. Now opening its doors as a place for physical therapy and rehabilitation, patients could participate in activities like woodworking, swimming, weaving, and more. During World War II, a section of the property was transformed to a U.S. military camp known as Camp Morrow. After the war, the hospitals held many long-term patients struggling from polio. By the 1950s, much of the 600 acres had sold, leaving the hospital with only 62 acres, which still functions as a hospital to this day.[5] Many of the remaining buildings have been abandoned since the 1980s, and many of the structures have since burned down or been removed by the city to make room for new developments. The buildings that do remain are now considered historic sites and are protected by security 24/7, although most are neglected and decaying. Rumors circulated that these buildings are left untouched due to hauntings from the patients who experienced the horrific treatment that is said to have taken place within the facility.[6]

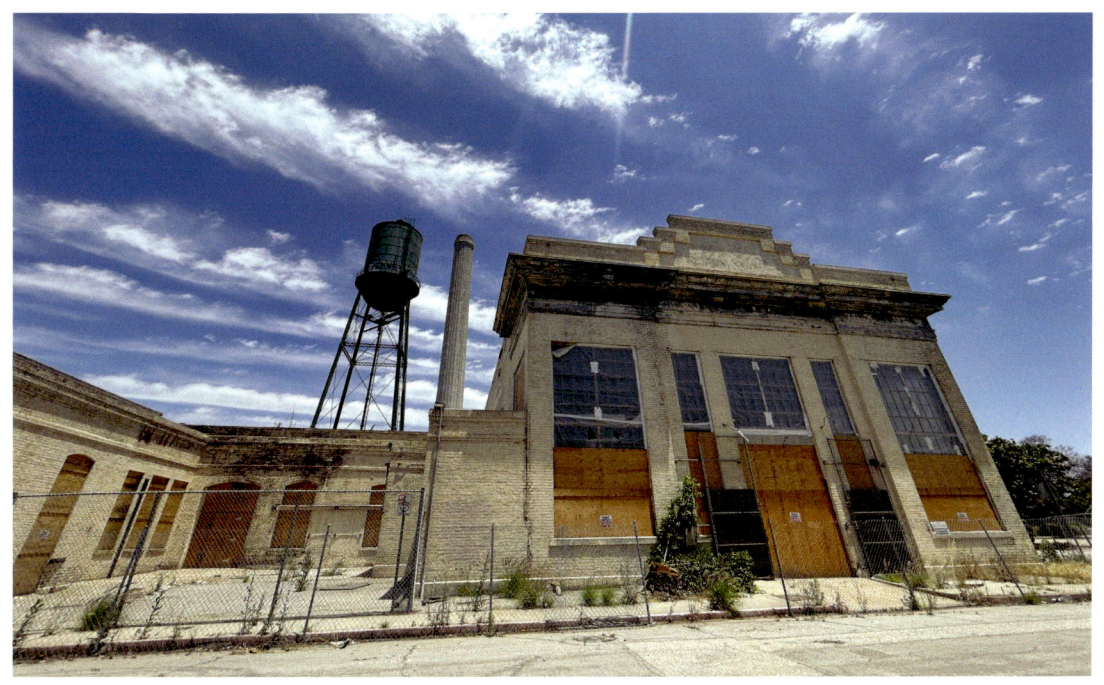

Dozens of abandoned buildings once sat at L.A. County Poor Farm, until recently when the property changed due to a huge fire in 2022 that damaged many structures beyond the point of repair.

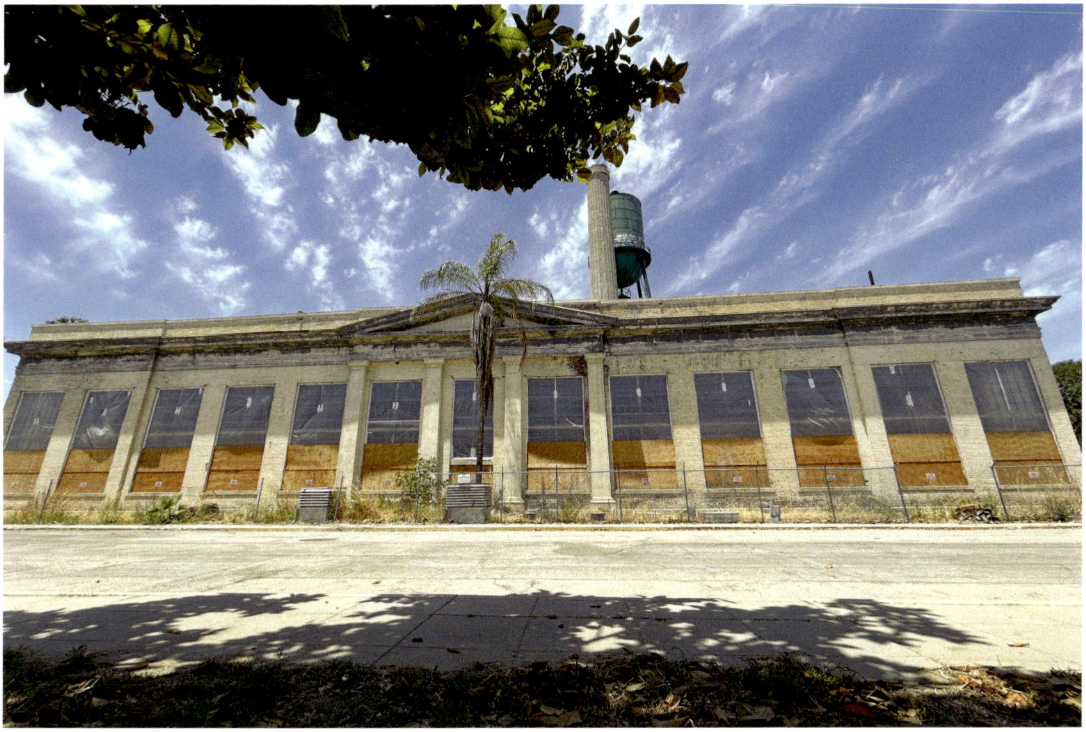

This power plant complex consisted of not only a powerhouse, but also a laundry room, icehouse, brine room, broiler room, and a telephone system.

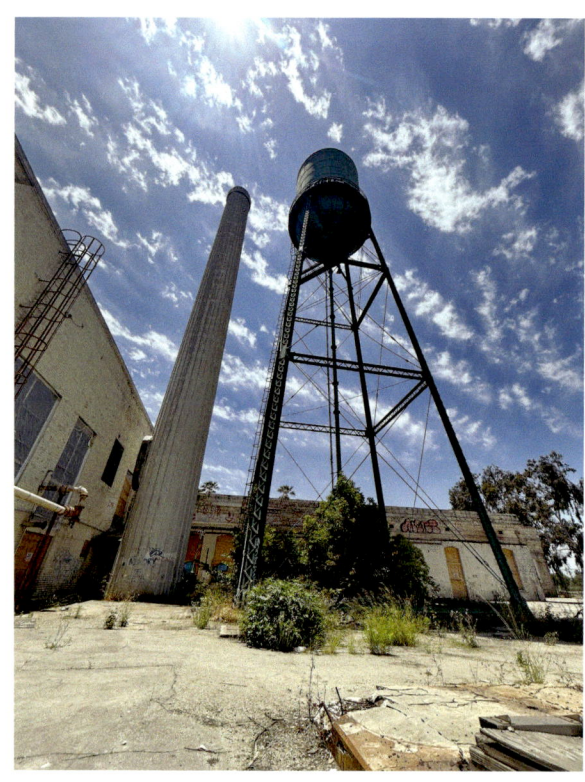

Left: This water tower was fed by the property's artisan well and supplied the entire compound with enough water for showers, drinking, gardening, and hundreds of livestock.

Below: Most of the buildings at Rancho Los Amigos were constructed in Spanish or brick Victorian-era institutional styles, including this structure which served as the men's psychiatric ward.

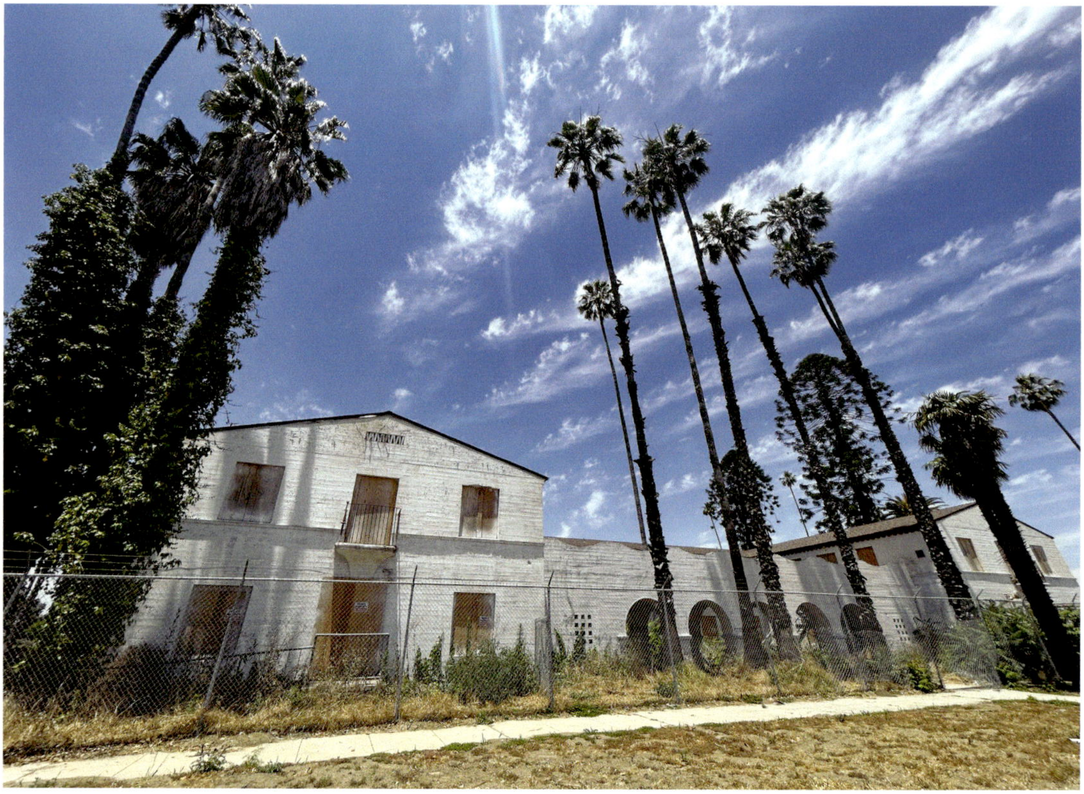

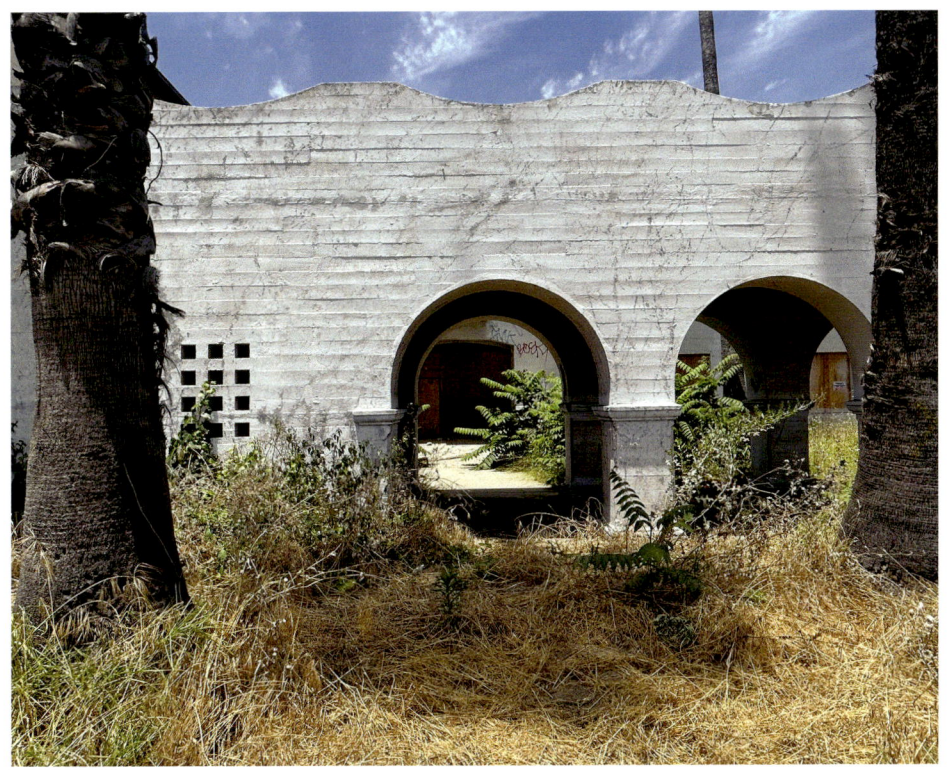

Above: Arch hallways surrounding a small courtyard at one of the few remaining structures since the fire in 2022 that destroyed over half of the abandoned buildings.

Right: Beautiful details of a tiny balcony on one of the buildings at the L.A. County Poor Farms' psych ward.

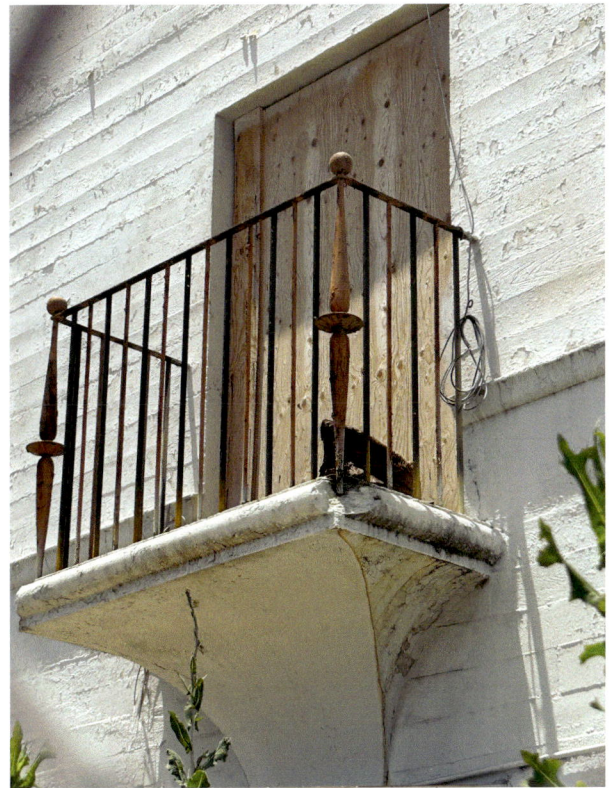

Wadsworth Chapel

Wadsworth Chapel was built in 1900 in what is now one of the most prestigious neighborhoods of Los Angeles. It is often referred to as the Catholic-Protestant Chapels because the structure consists of two separate chapels. The once-thriving chapel also spent several years as a community center, where locals would gather to participate in a variety of activities including recreational programs, educational courses, and support groups. The Victorian-style structure was forced to close due to lack of funding needed to repair the extensive damage caused by the 1971 Sylmar earthquake. The gorgeous chapel sits directly at the entrance of the West Los Angeles VA Campus, where it remains untouched, protected but completely uninhabitable.

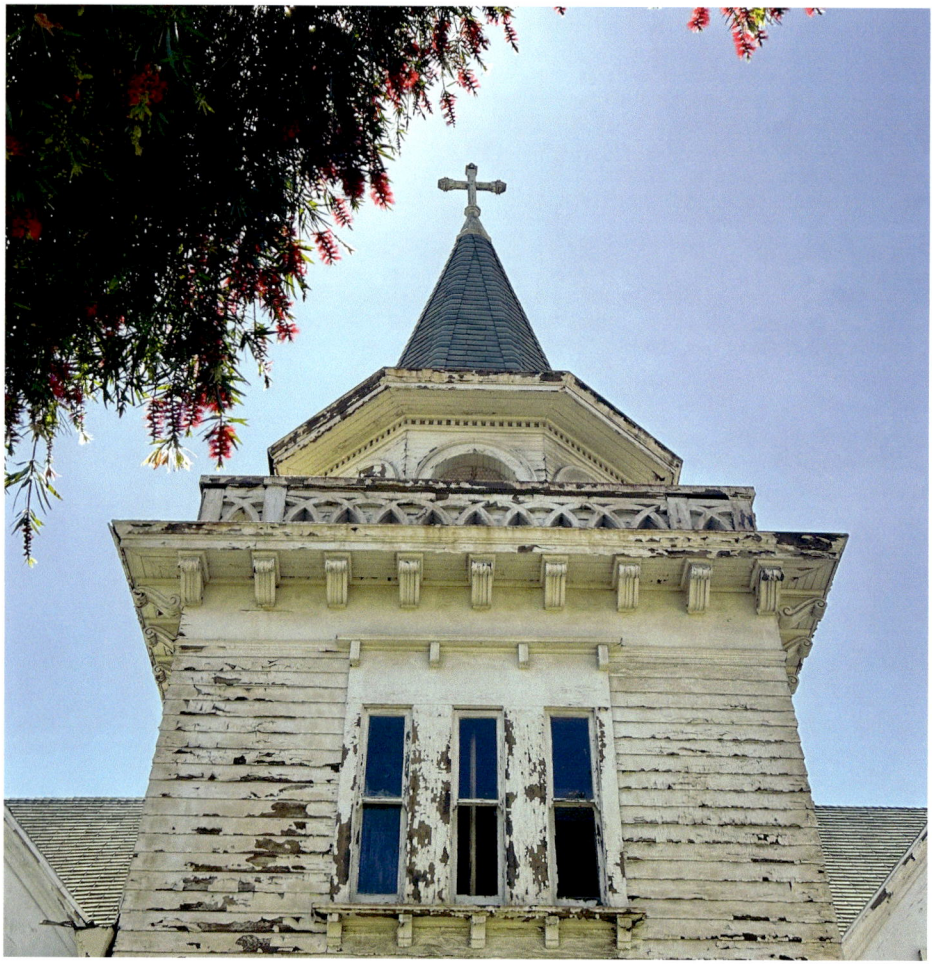

Gazing at Wadsworth Chapel through a crimson bottle-brush tree to view one of the chapel's many beautiful spires.

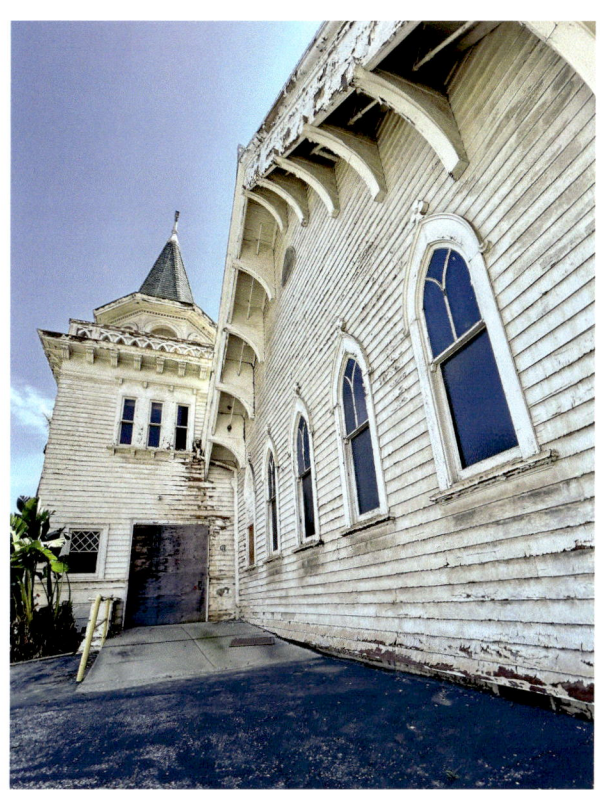

The back entrance of Wadsworth Chapel has been welded shut to protect the structure from vandalism.

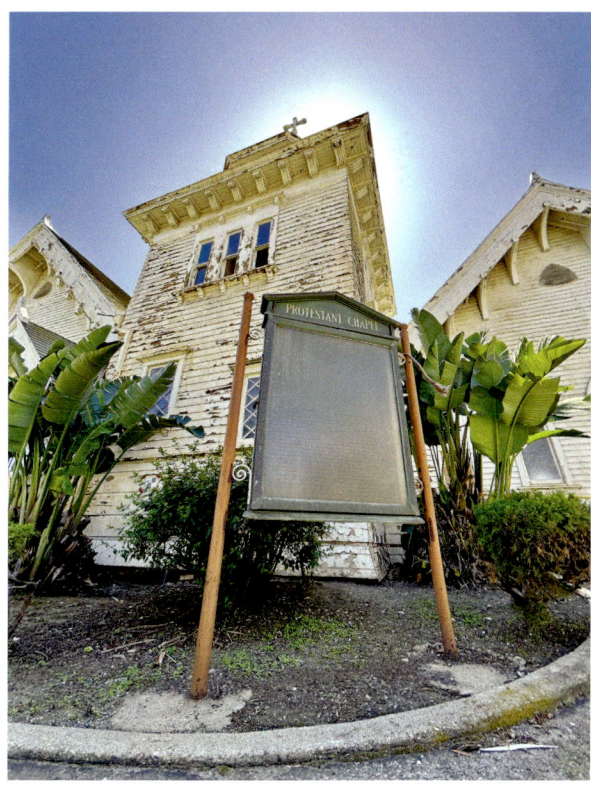

The bulletin board outside of the back entrance, which once posted chapel events, community gatherings, and services.

Sunken City Ruins

San Pedro is one of the furthest neighborhoods in Los Angeles, California, known mainly for its cliffside coastal views, its giant fish market, and the famous Sunken City Ruins. It all started early January 2, 1929, when the shifting of the earth led to giant cracks running throughout the streets, barely missing some of the cliffside bungalows.

Shortly after, engineers monitoring the cracks noted a lateral movement of 8 inches and vertical drop of 3 inches—just enough to cause a quick sense of panic to the nearby homeowners, with many deciding to move out quickly to avoid the destruction.[7] It was not long before the city engineers realized that the predicted landslide was inevitable, and the land was roped off to the public and left abandoned for good. Surrounded by an 8-foot iron fence, most of the cement has fallen into the sea, yet what does remain has become a popular site for artists, photographers, and explorers alike.

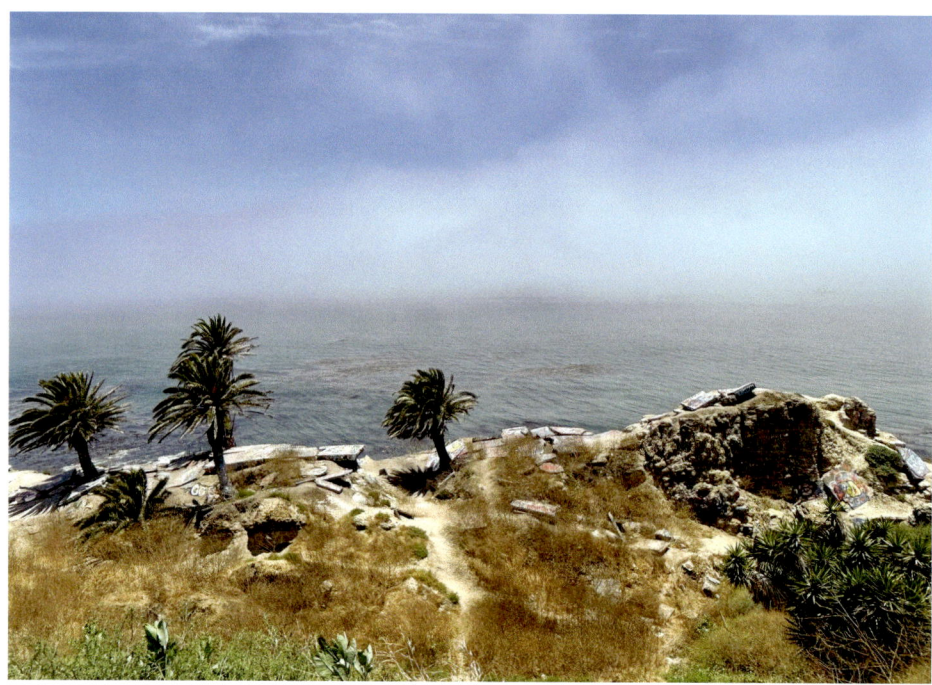

When you first approach the disaster site, it looks as if it is just a cement lot falling away into the sea, but it was once a quaint and exclusive neighborhood.

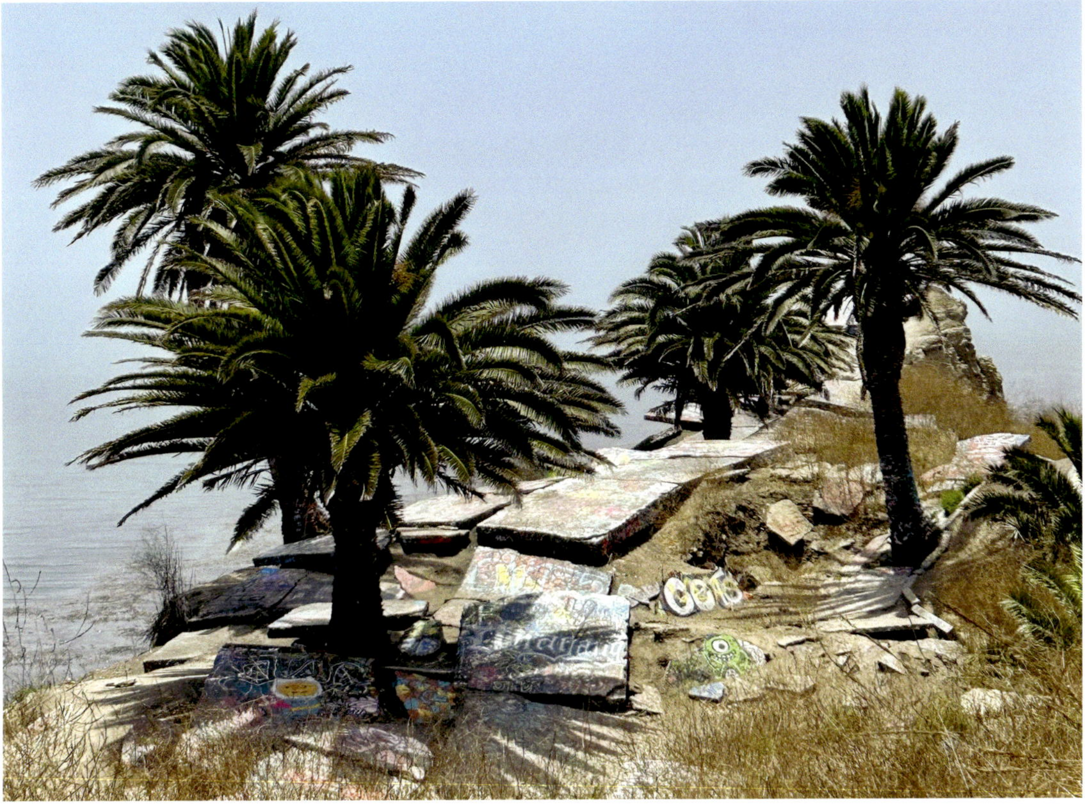

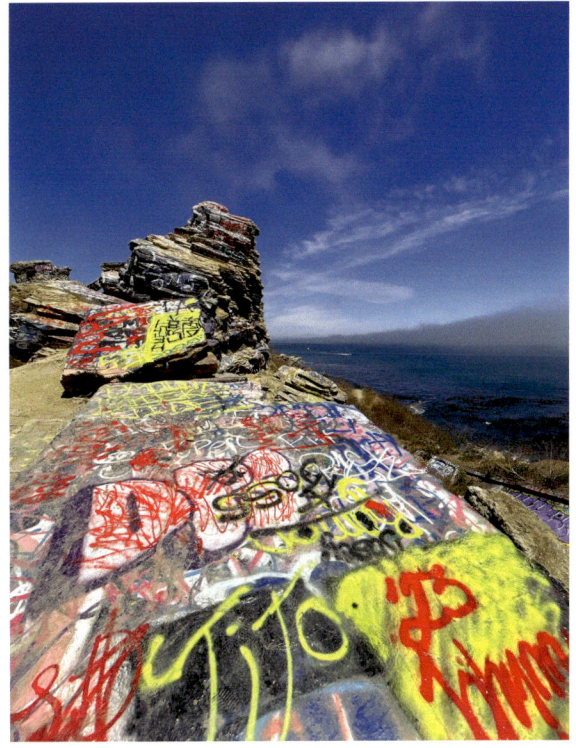

Above: All that remains are the huge slabs of concrete and palm trees that seem to be barely holding on to sidewalks they used to line.

Right: Graffiti covers almost everything in sight, and the remains resemble a post-apocalyptic movie set.

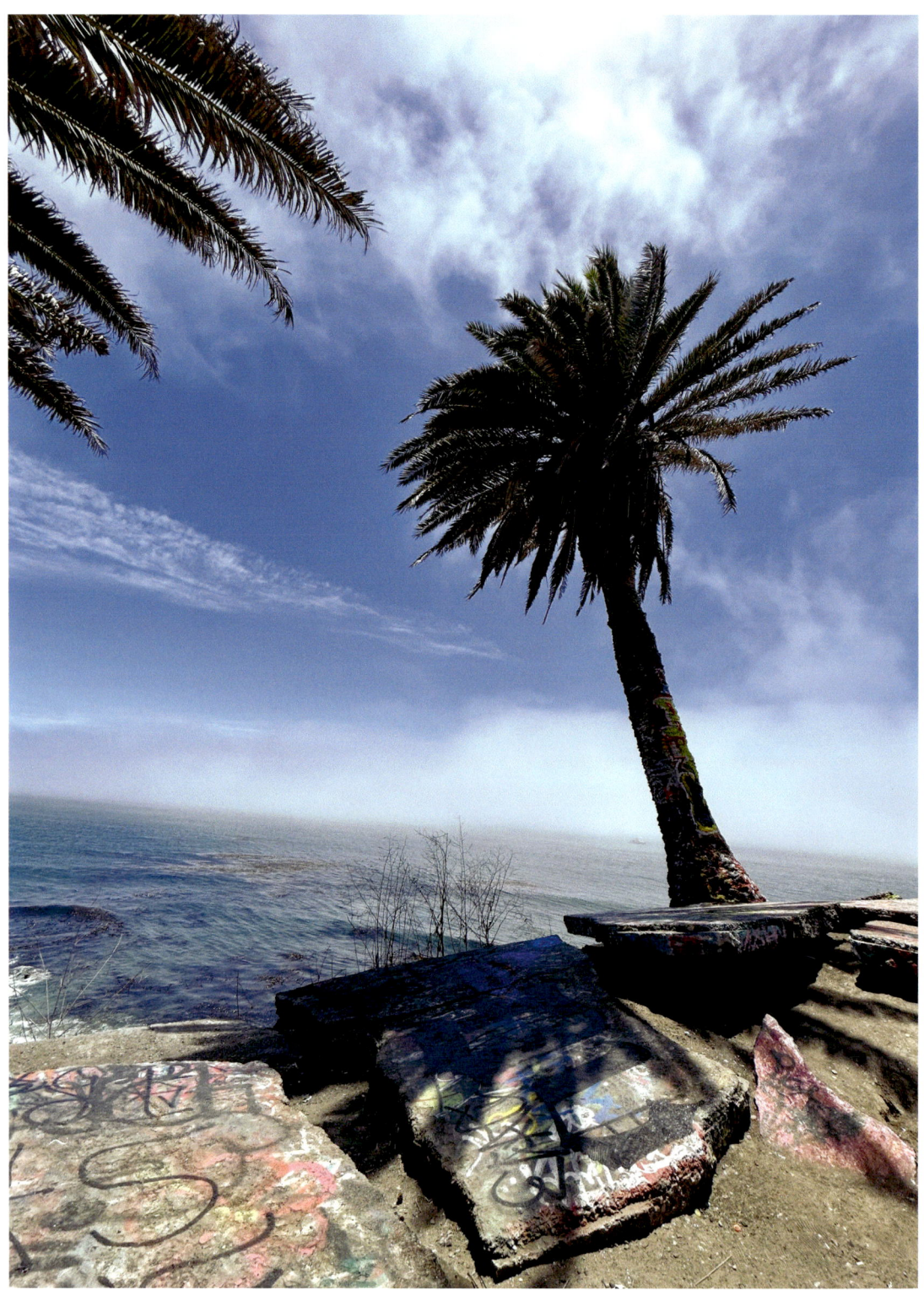

Palm trees are the most common tree remaining in the sunken city disaster site, and although they are not native to this area, this is very common for neighborhoods across California, especially beach-front properties.

2

SANTA MONICA MOUNTAIN RUINS

The beautiful Santa Monica Mountains are one of the most diverse mountain ranges in all of Los Angeles County, with a lush landscape covering approximately 56 miles of coastal wilderness. This area has a huge state park and many gorgeous hiking trails throughout the winding canyons, so whether you prefer hiking into historic ruins or through creepy forgotten places, then the Santa Monica Mountains is the perfect destination for a day of exploring. Each site is unique, quirky, and full of history, making Santa Monica more than just a trendy beach town, but a playground for urban explorers.

Murphy's Ranch

Not all ruins have a joyful history, one example is the eerie remnants of one of L.A.'s most famous abandoned locations: Murphy's Ranch. Tucked deep within the canyon are the ruins of a mysterious compound thought to have been built by Nazi sympathizers. This location has a lot of stories floating around the internet, but no one really knows for sure what the intentions were behind this once self-sufficient compound. Follow me down 524 cement steps to the ruins of a place once known as Murphy's Ranch.

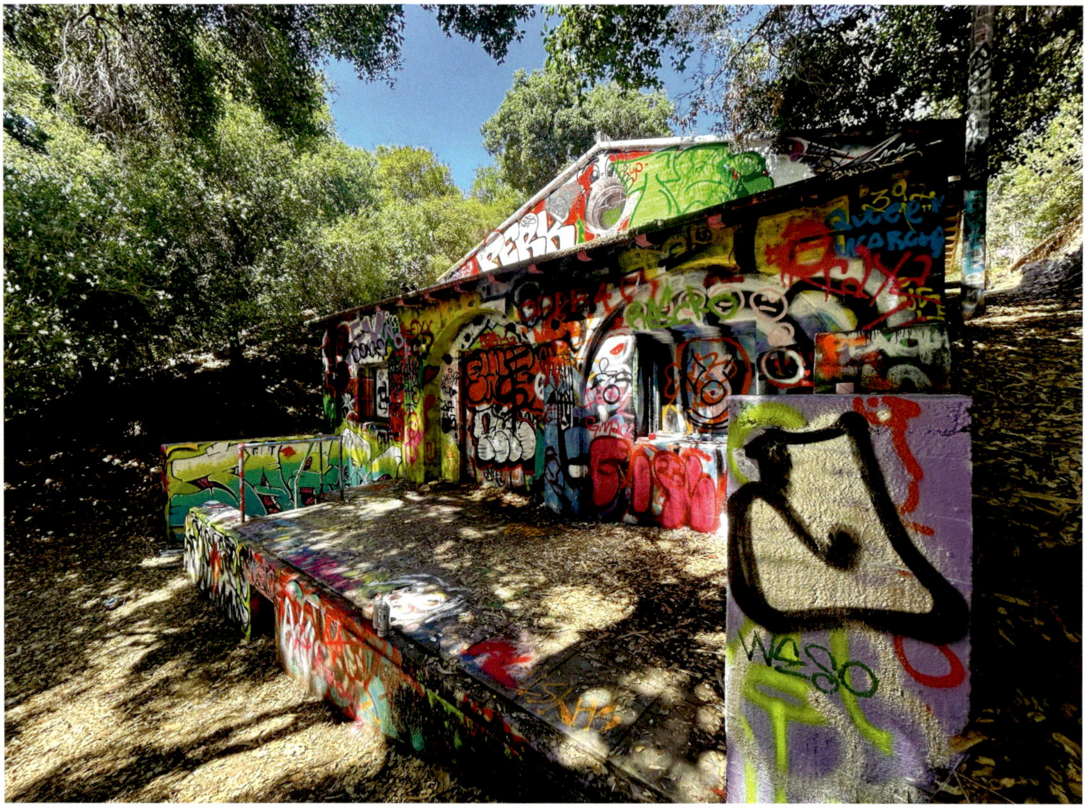

Above: The powerhouse is one of the only things left standing after the several fires, earthquakes, and city-ordered demolitions.

Left: All windows and doors have been welded shut to prevent any injuries from happening inside of the powerhouse.

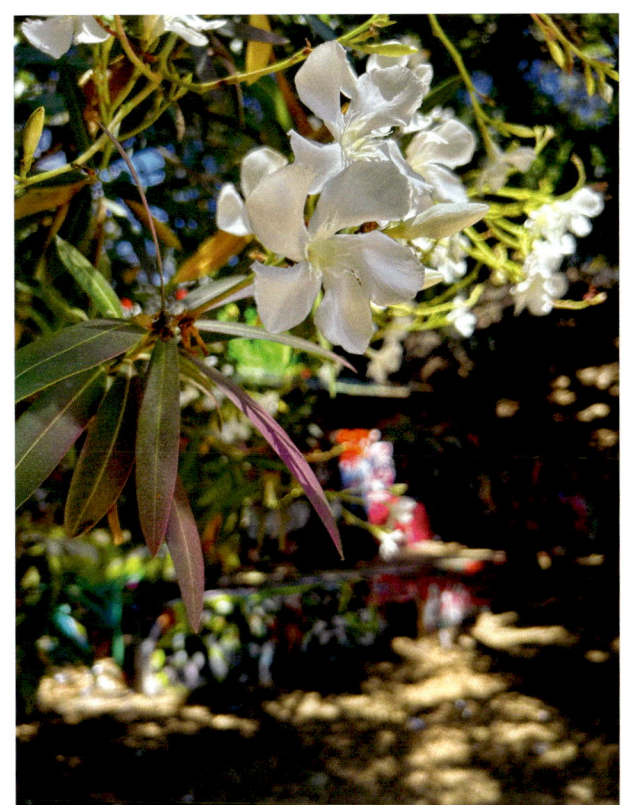

Right: Many flowers and exotic plants still bloom around the property because of the moisture in the air from the nearby creek and ocean.

Below: Every inch of cement in the compound is now covered in layers of graffiti.

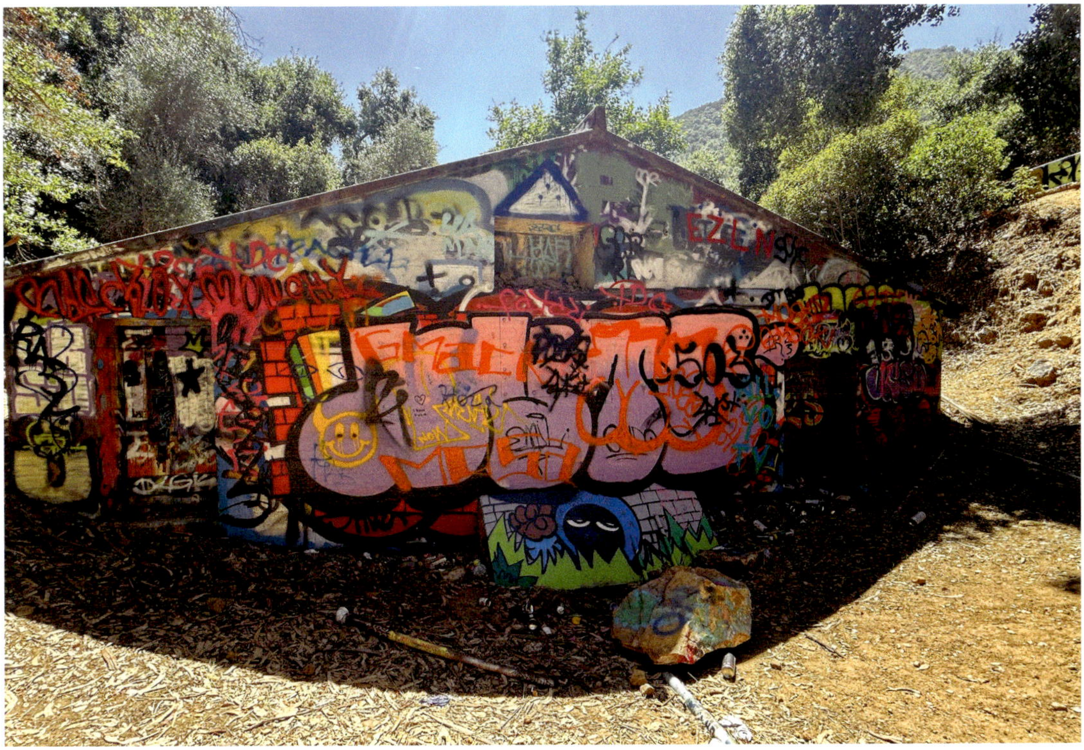

In 1933, the 50-acre property was purchased by a man under the alias of Jessie Murphy. Historians believe that this man was in truth an agent for Nazi Germany named *Herr* Schmidt. It is said that Schmidt came to America to build a complex that could house other pro-Nazi sympathizers and their families safely until Hitler defeated America, and they could surface to help convert the country into a Nazi society. The blueprint that was designed consisted of a four-story mansion with beautiful landscaping, twenty-two bedrooms, servant quarters, multiple vegetable gardens, as well as a cattle barn, giant water tank, fuel tank, bomb shelter, and even its own power station. Soon the property was home to many Silver Shirts and pro-Nazi followers who helped with the ongoing construction, daily upkeep, and the securing of the property. As we all know, the war ended, and the group's dream of the Nazi takeover was never carried out. On December 8, 1941, the ranch was raided by the FBI and over fifty residents were taken from the property and put into custody, including the man who started it all, *Herr* Schmidt. By 1948, everyone had been released and Schmidt decided to sell the property to the Huntington Hartford Foundation, who then transformed the property into an artists' colony which remained functional until it closed in 1965.[1] The land and the remaining structures stood abandoned until it was bought by the city of Los Angeles ten years later.

The first time I ever visited Murphy's Ranch, many of the ruins were still standing. Unfortunately, over the years, many explorers were injured, and due to multiple rescues taking place, the city of Los Angeles decided to knock down and remove many of the dilapidated ruins. Now, all that remains are the stairs which were once patrolled, the boarded-up powerhouse, a collapsed barn, damaged water tanks, and scattered, rusted appliances. Its history was never confirmed and is still one of the most mysterious and eerie places in L.A.

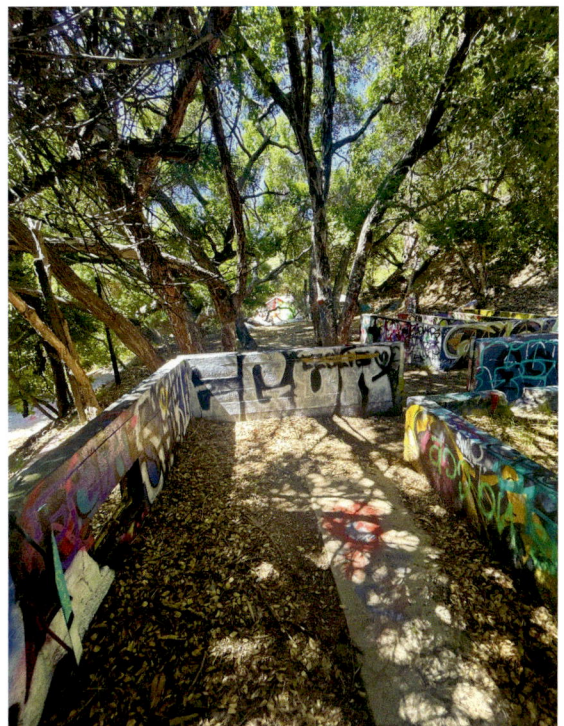

Right: The property had over twelve raised garden beds that are still visible today and mainly overgrown with weeds.

Below: Judging by the entrance to this garden, I believe this may have been a greenhouse at one time.

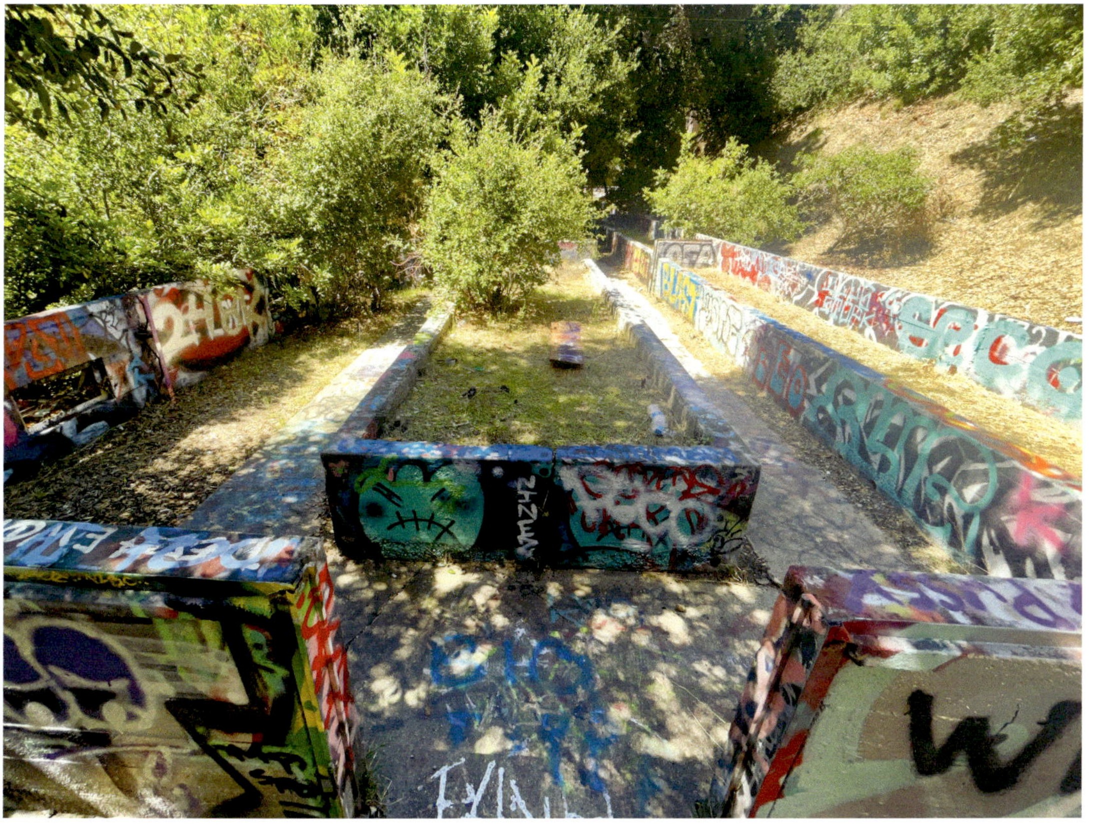

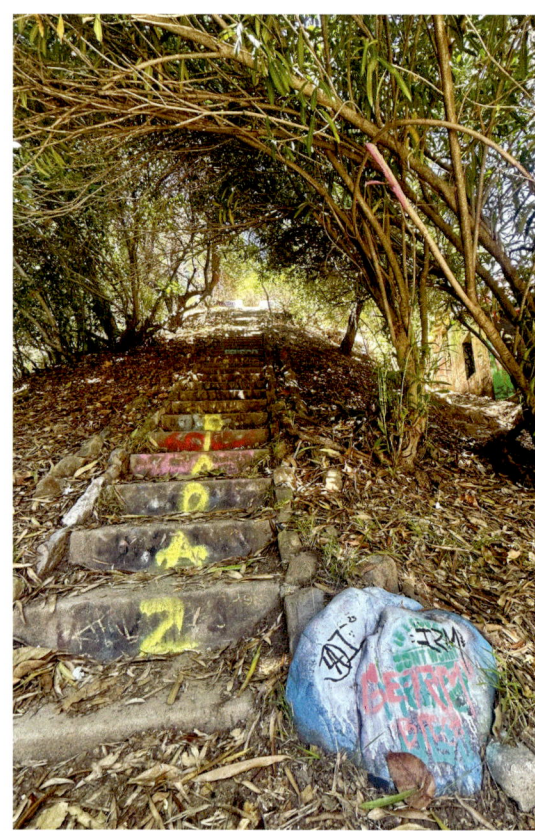

Left: The Murphy Ranch property grounds have over five sets of staircases, each consisting of over 500 steps.

Below left: These staircases were once used by the compounds guards to assist them in patrolling the grounds from a higher view.

Below right: At the top of the hill sits a giant, 375,000-gallon water tank with a beautiful view of Santa Monica Beach.

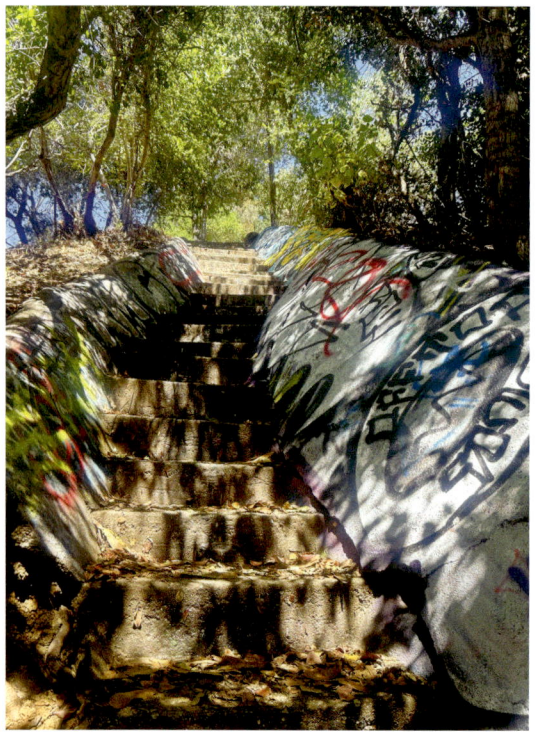

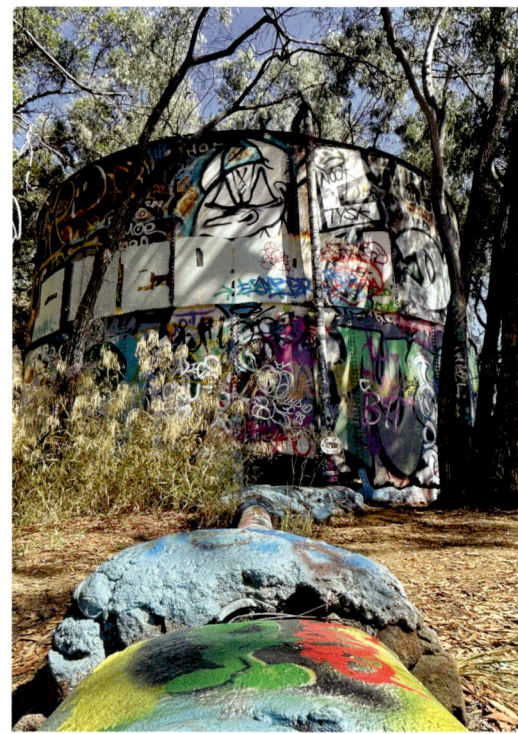

Solstice Canyon

Solstice Canyon is a beautiful canyon, full of stunning hiking trails, a clear stream fed by a waterfall, and multiple historic ruins, so it is no wonder why this trail is so popular among hikers and urban explorers. These mountains are rich in history, once being home to both Chumash and Tongva natives, and as time progressed, many homesteaders and explorers lived, worked, and traveled through the mountain's hidden valleys and canyons, leaving behind bits and pieces of their lifestyles for us to study for decades. In fact, Santa Monica is home to many abandoned sites that are open to the public to explore, one of which is the oldest structure within these canyons; only half a mile from the ruins of one family's oasis dream home sits the skeleton of the historic Keller House, dating back to 1865. The land was bought by a famous Los Angeles wine merchant named William Keller, and a hunting cabin was built. The cabin was no match for the wildfires that repeatedly hit the area, and soon the rock structure was built in hopes of being able to survive most natural disasters. Ultimately, the land was doomed, and no home would ever thrive in this canyon.

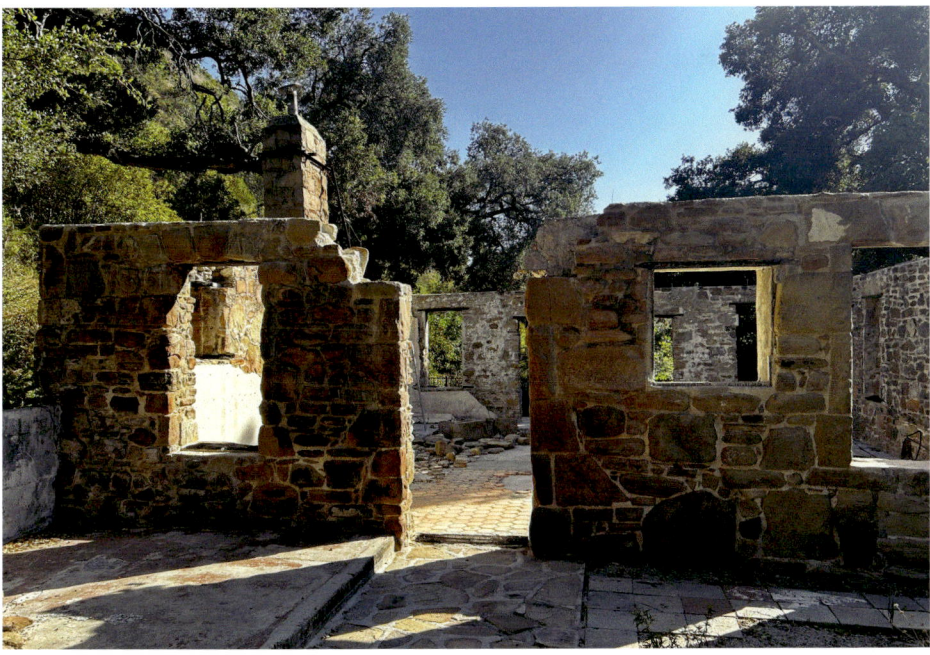

The historic Keller House is one of L.A.'s oldest homes. Although not much remains, it is still protected by cameras and a steel fence because the ruins play a very important role in California's history.

Just a short walk from the Keller House is another ruin of one family's dream retirement home. In 1952, Fred and Florence Roberts commissioned an architect to design the home of their dreams. Built of stone, brick, and wood, the home was constructed to flow with the natural curvatures of the surrounding rocks and streams, with views of small waterfalls and lush tropical landscape right outside of the windows. Unfortunately, after only thirty years, the gorgeous home was burned down by the Dayton Canyon Fire.[2] The devastation of the fire left the home with only fireplaces, concrete slabs, and few exterior walls. What was once a grand estate is now reduced to ruins but can still be accessed and appreciated at the end of Solstice Canyon Trail.

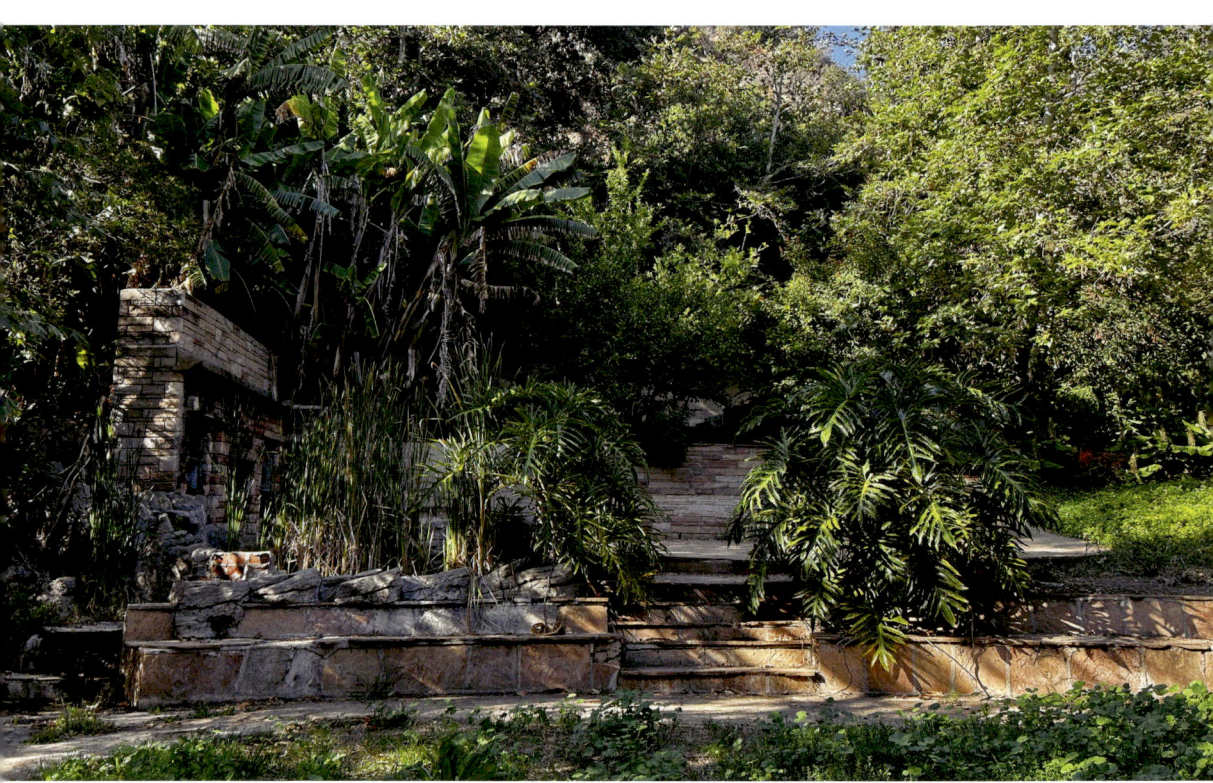

Approaching what would have been the front entrance to the beautiful Roberts family's tropical estate.

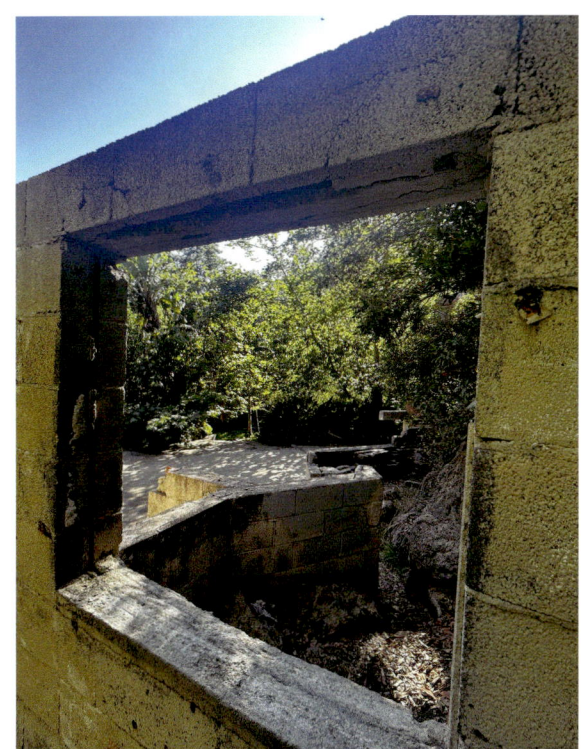

Right: Gazing through one of the three remaining window frames at the ruins of the Roberts' family home.

Below: Large open-floor plan for what was once a beautiful kitchen. Behind the dining area, there was once a window so one could enjoy looking out to see the flowing creek and small waterfall directly behind the home.

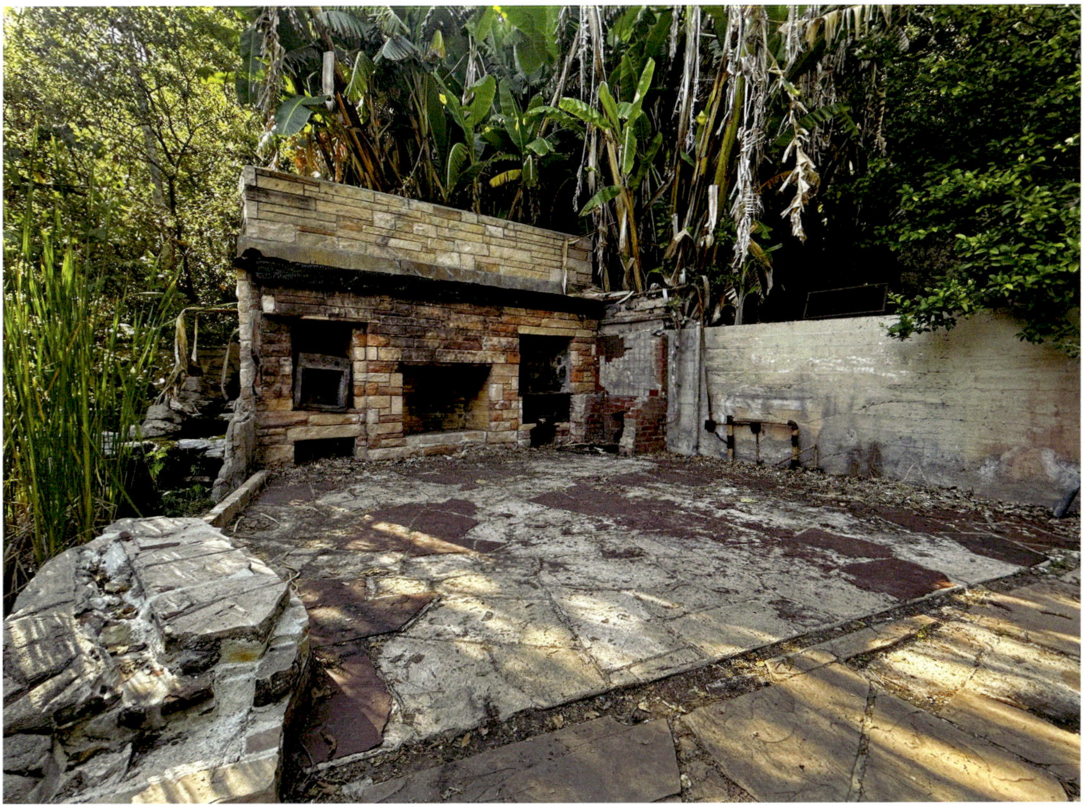

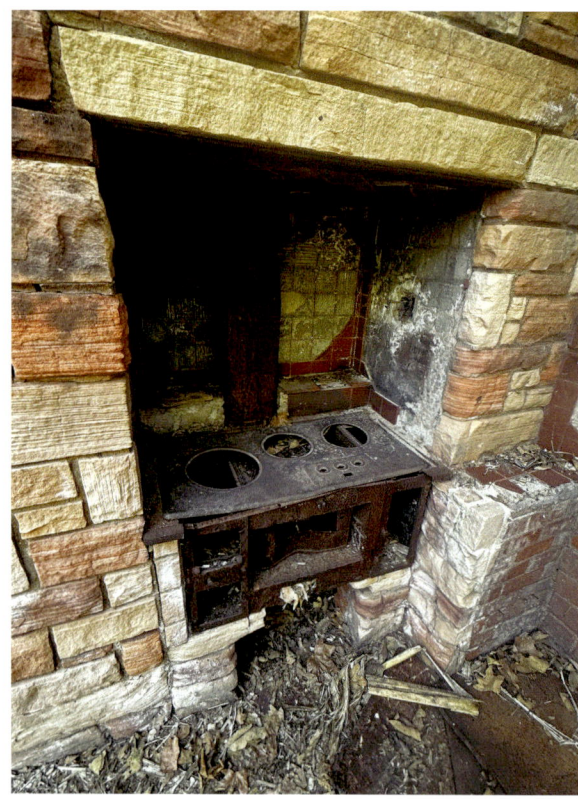

An old, rusted stove top and oven remain next to one of many lavish fireplaces on the property.

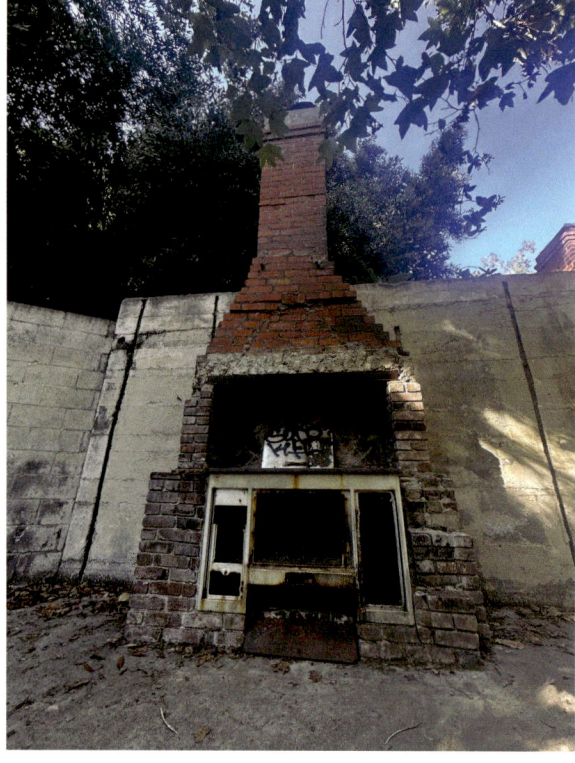

The largest stove remains built into this giant fireplace which has survived the multiple natural disasters that have hit this location.

Notice the lush tropical plants are still thriving due to the layout of the irrigation system that is being fed by the nearby creek.

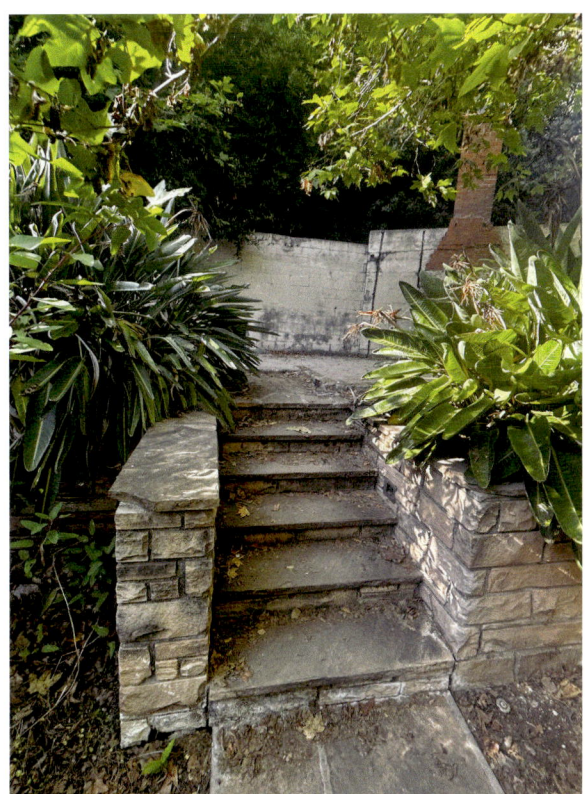

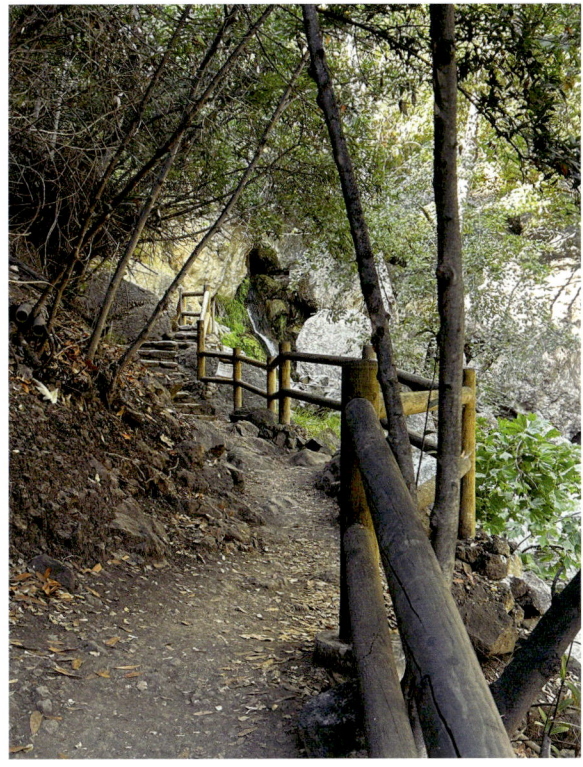

The nature trail that Fred Roberts constructed with his family gave them easy access to the largest waterfall behind their property.

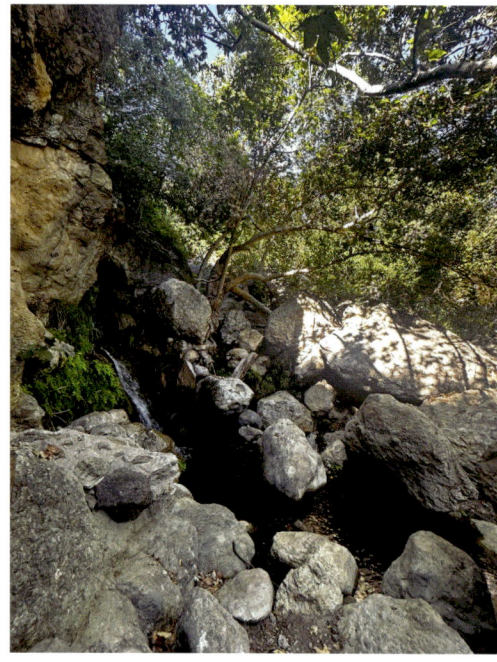

Although the waterfall does not look like much here, after heavy rainfall, it is much more powerful. If you look closely, you can see a cement deck that was once used for the family and guests to lounge and view the waterfall.

Topanga Canyon

Topanga Canyon is a very popular route for beachgoers, artists, and hippies to enjoy a beautiful sunny day in California. Its unique and bohemian history has set this road apart from other canyon roads in the area. Creative homes, art walls, quirky stores, and scenic views are a few reasons this road is so special. Hidden behind the oak trees sits the mysterious ruins of a partially built house with a dark past, only accessible by the steel beams from an old bridge: "The Canned Heat Suicide House." The property was rumored to be owned by Bob Hite, the lead singer of a popular rock band called Canned Heat, and the home was said to be occupied by him and his band mates for many years. On September 3, 1970, one of the members of the band, Alan "Blind Owl" Wilson, was found dead on the hillside behind Bob's house. The cause of death for the twenty-seven-year-old musician was determined to be barbiturate overdose.[3] Many people who knew the young man believe that it may have been an intentional suicide because Alan had been battling severe depression for many months prior to the incident. Several years later, the home was destroyed by a flood. In 1990, they attempted to build a new structure, but construction was halted due to more extreme flooding. They soon realized that this desirable location was a hazardous flood plain, and the structure has remained abandoned for over thirty years, slowly being reclaimed to nature.

Right: Metal beams that once supported the driveway to the Canned House are now just a plank for curious explorers desperate enough to cross.

Below: After heavy rainfall, the creek flows very rapidly, making it almost impossible to cross without scaling the steel beams.

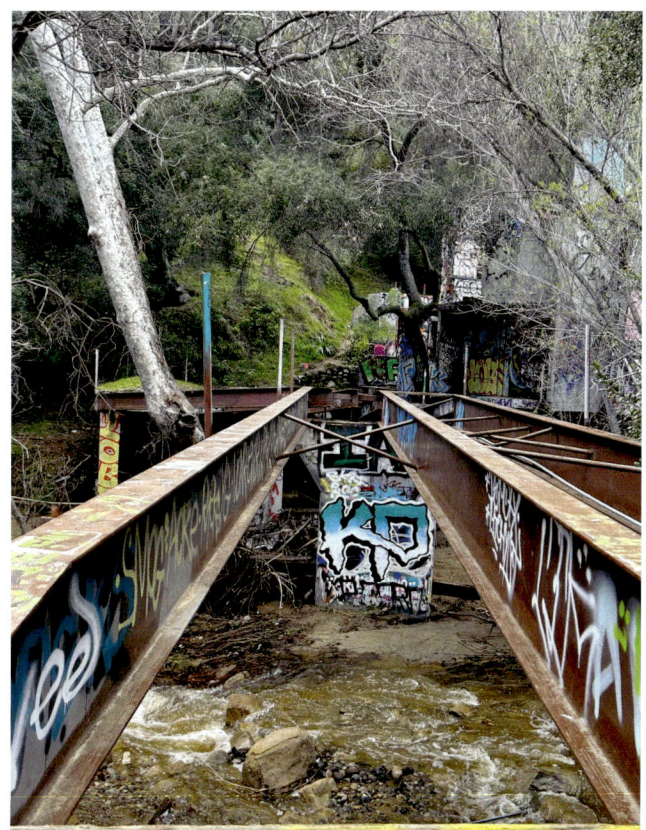

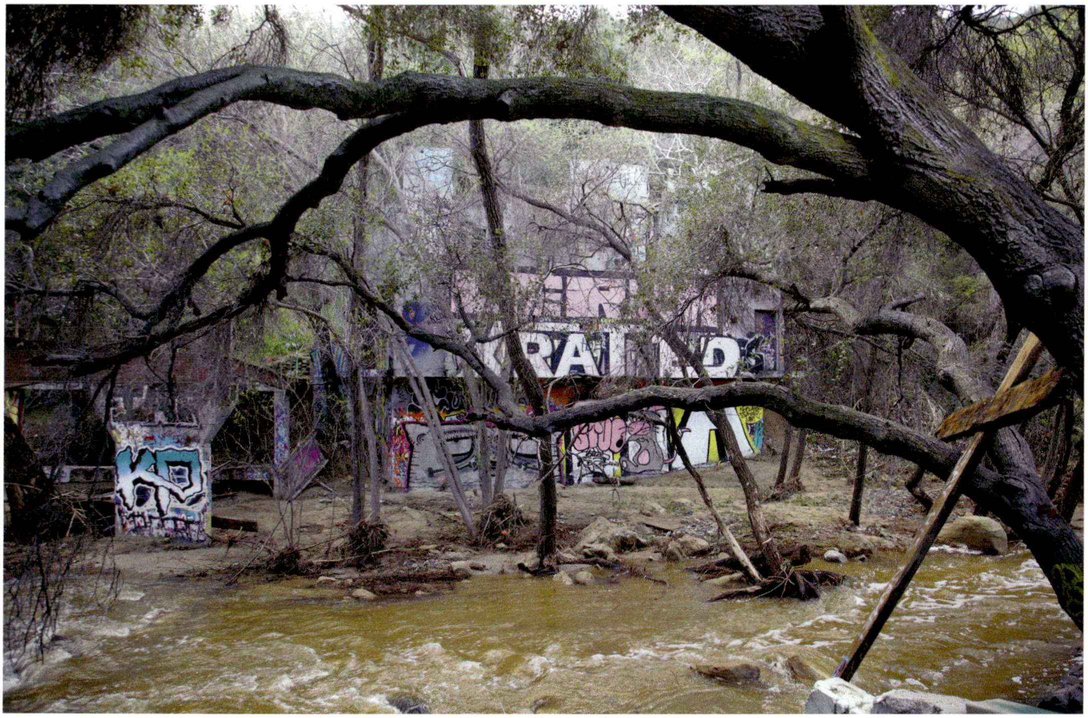

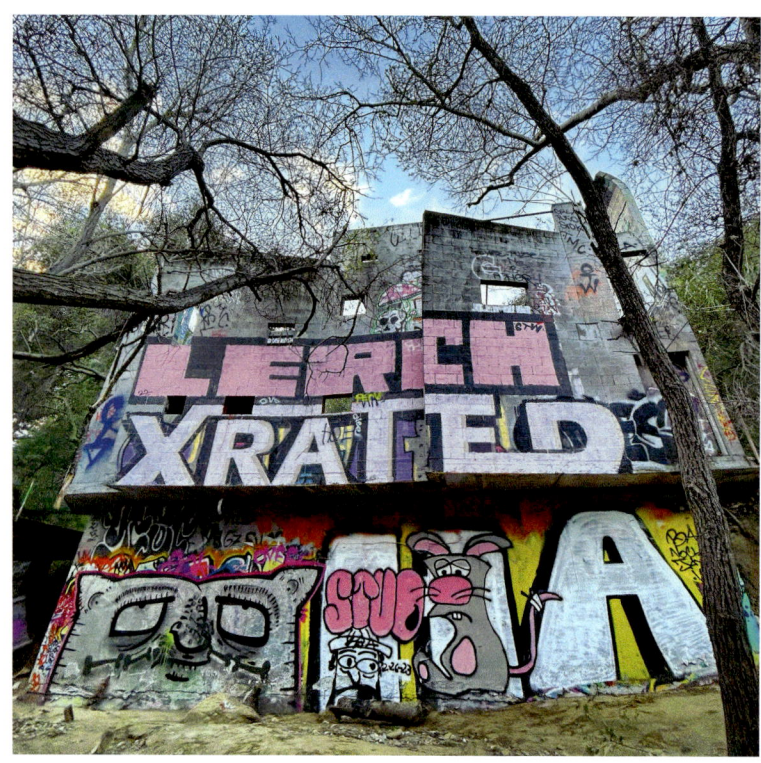

Left: Although its design is often mistaken for nearly collapsing, the front wall of this home was constructed to look as if it was being peeled off.

Below: Construction on the house was never completed, but what progress was made is now crumbling into the creek below.

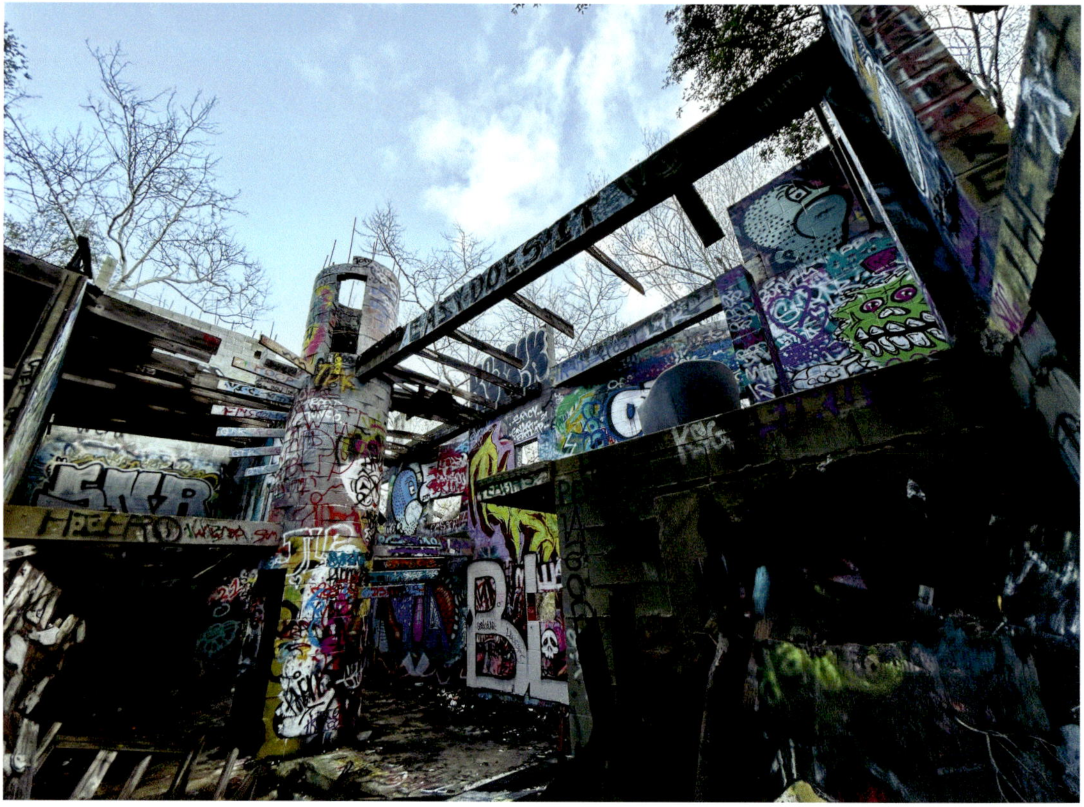

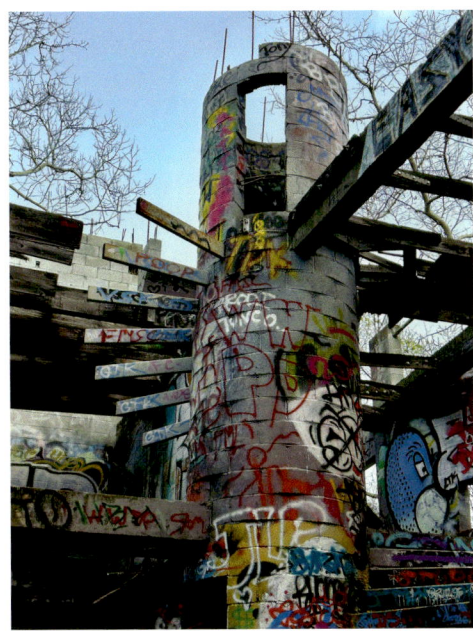 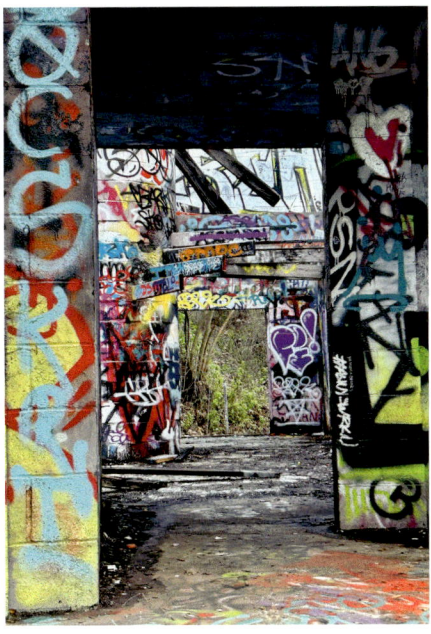

Above left: The spiral staircase is perhaps the most famous structural design incorporated in the ruins of Canned Heat's dream home.

Above right: From the outside looking in, all you can see is colorful graffiti scribbles on the walls and entryways.

Below: Looking up through the holes in the floor of what would have been the third story of the Canned Heat house.

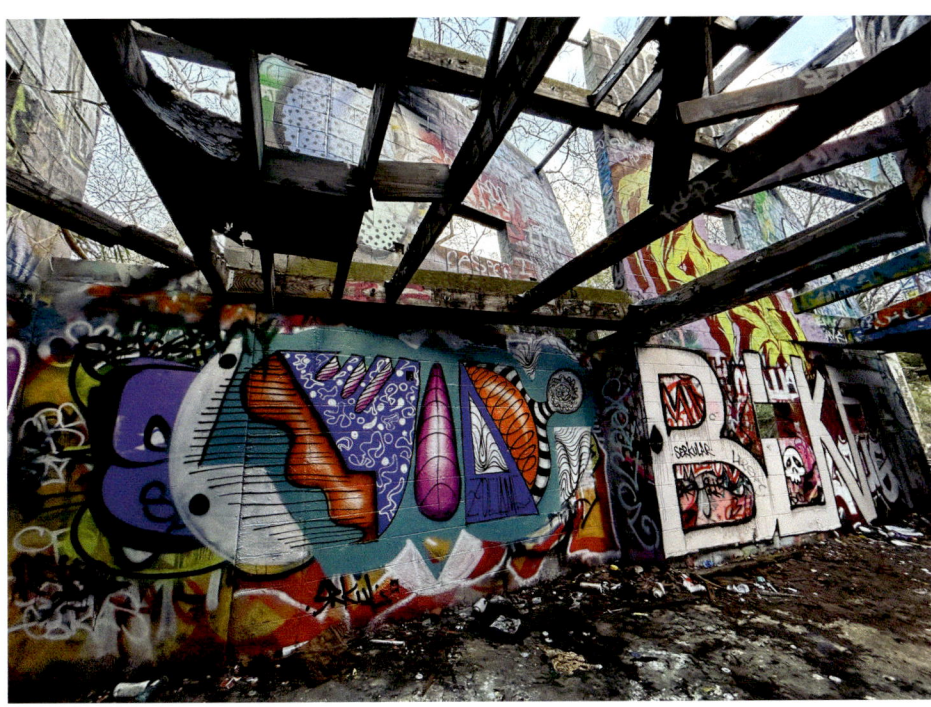

3

SILVER, GOLD, AND OIL MINES OF L.A. COUNTY

Mentryville

Almost 100 years before Santa Clarita finally became a city, the small town of Mentryville was developed. Now it is the only ghost town left in Los Angeles County, tucked away in the Santa Susana Mountains on the edge of the Santa Clarita Valley, in what was once a booming oil drilling town. It was originally founded in 1876 by a man named Charles Mentry. He began building his dream of Mentryville and that dream grew to be a thriving town.[1]

It consisted of a thirteen-room mansion for Mr. Mentry and his family, as well as a barn, schoolhouse, bakery, bunkhouses, and cabins for the other workers. On a beautiful piece of land surrounded by rolling hills and oak trees, it was truly a place that people enjoyed calling home. Unfortunately, like many ghost towns across the state, it did not supply a profitable amount for long. In the early 1900s, Mentryville began to see its downfall. Charles Mentry shortly died from kidney disease in October 1900. The town was slowly abandoned, and by 1969, only the caretaker remained. In 1990, oil mining officially ceased. Today, Mentryville is recognized as Historical Landmark Marker 156-2 and has seen many restorations, although nothing is currently occupying any of the remaining buildings.

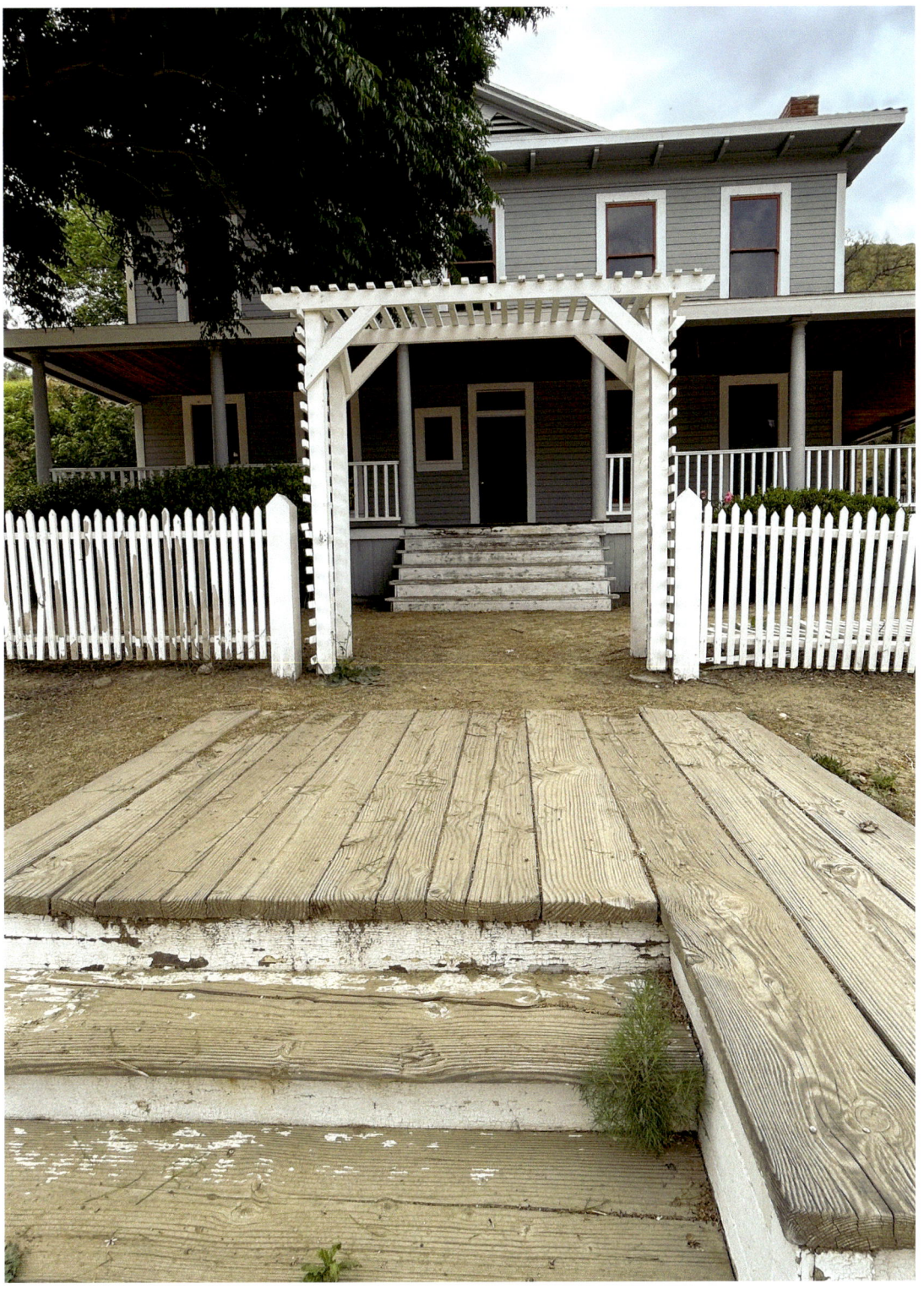

Built in 1899, the mansion at Mentryville had twelve bedrooms and was occupied by several different families throughout its time.

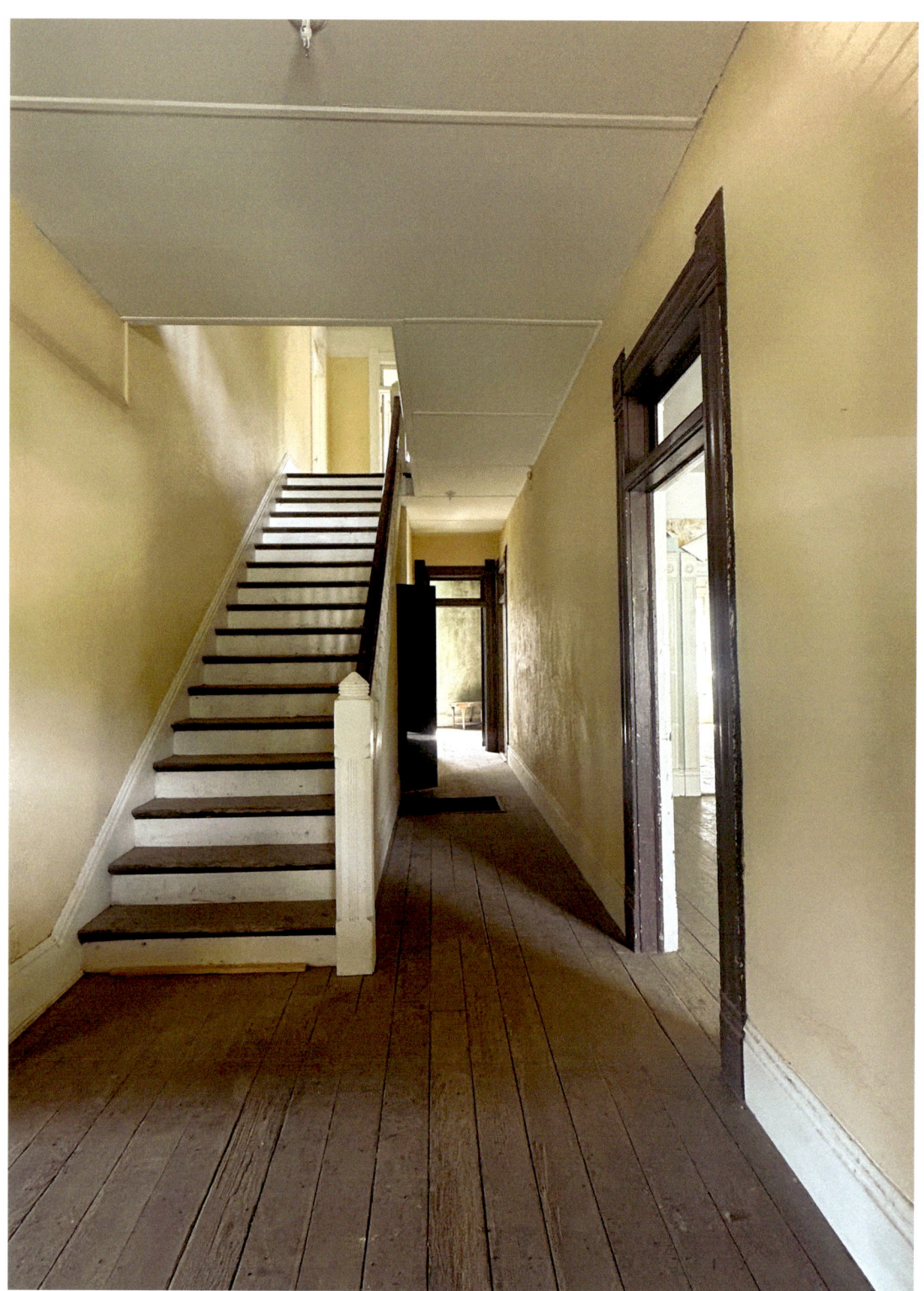

The home is now permanently closed, but the surrounding grounds are maintained by the caretaker are you are welcome to explore the land and view the structures from outside.

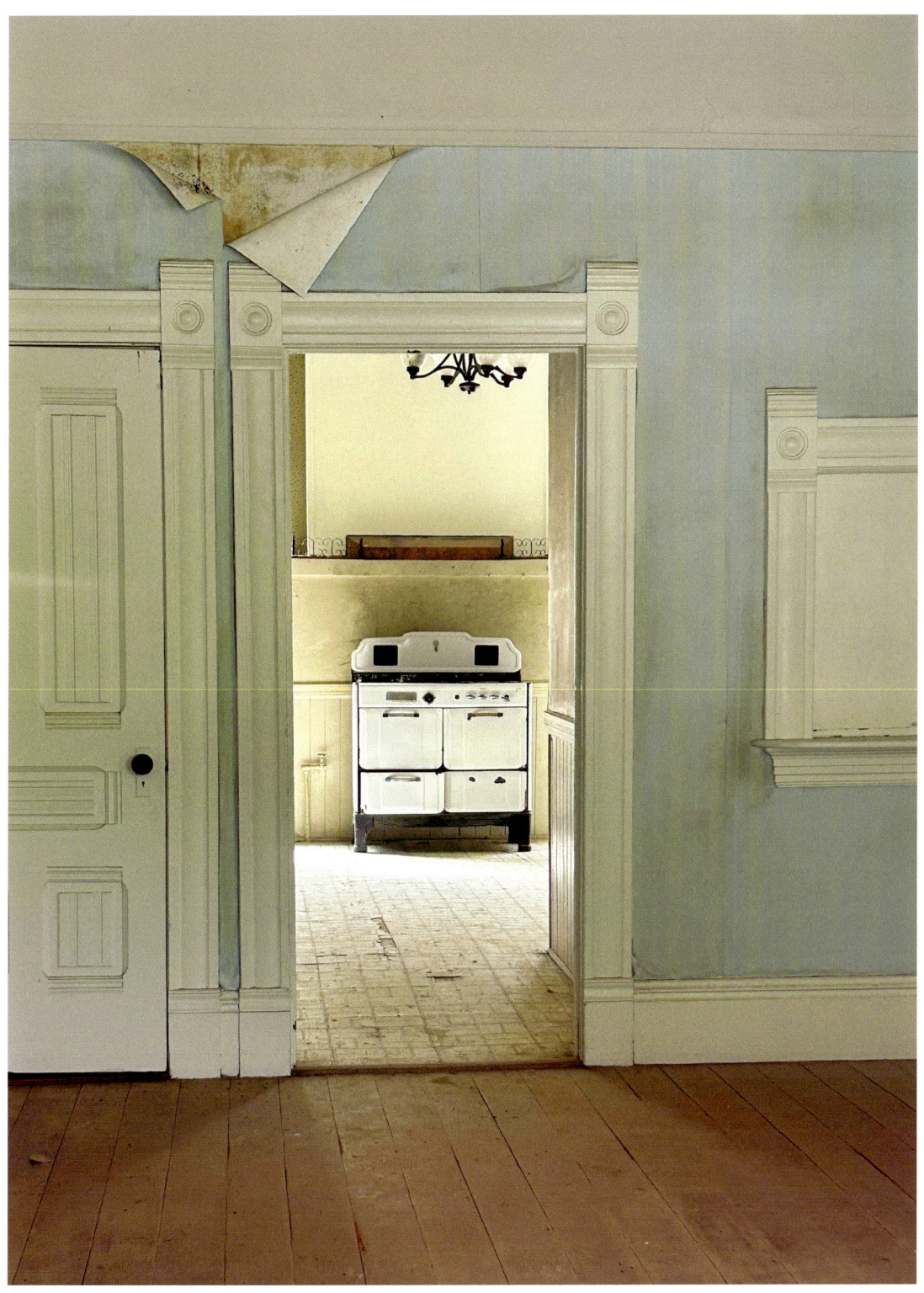

Although the Mentryville home is currently completely empty, the caretaker informed me that he is pushing for the city to allow them to transform this space into a museum.

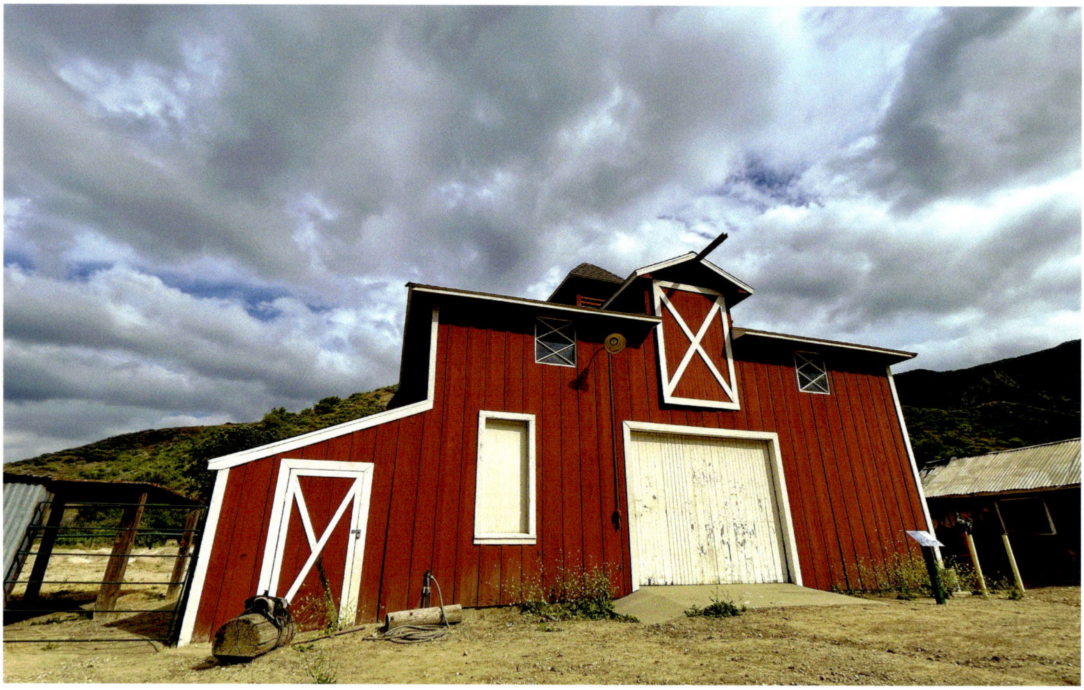

The barn has been restored several times and is the oldest standing structure remaining in Mentryville, built in 1890.

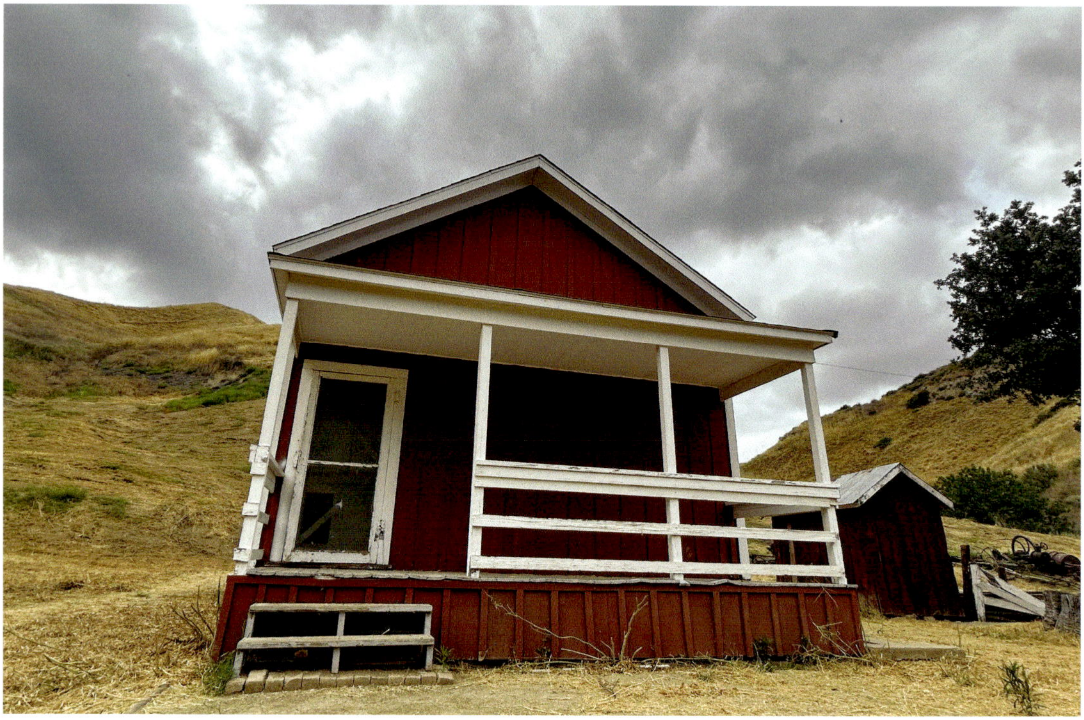

Mentryville's one-room schoolhouse was the very first schoolhouse in the Santa Clairita Valley and is still standing at its original location.

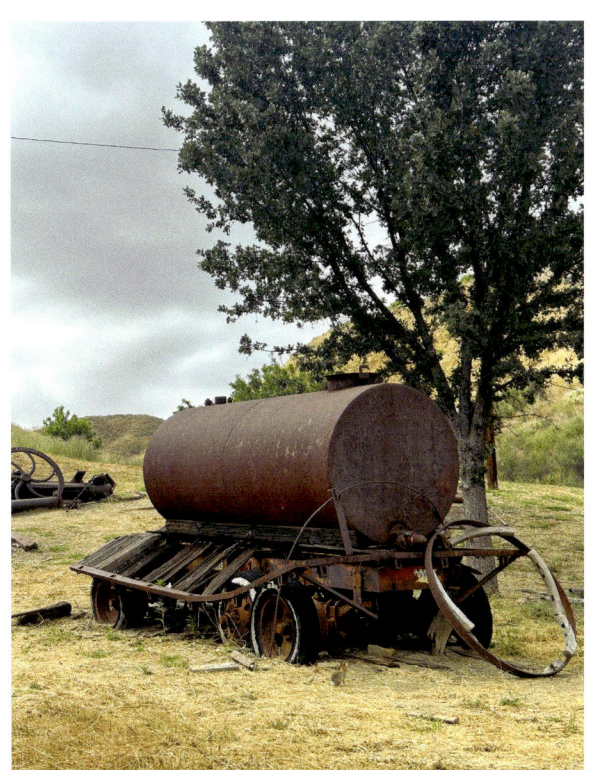

This tank once held the oil that was mined directly from the hills surrounding Mentryville.

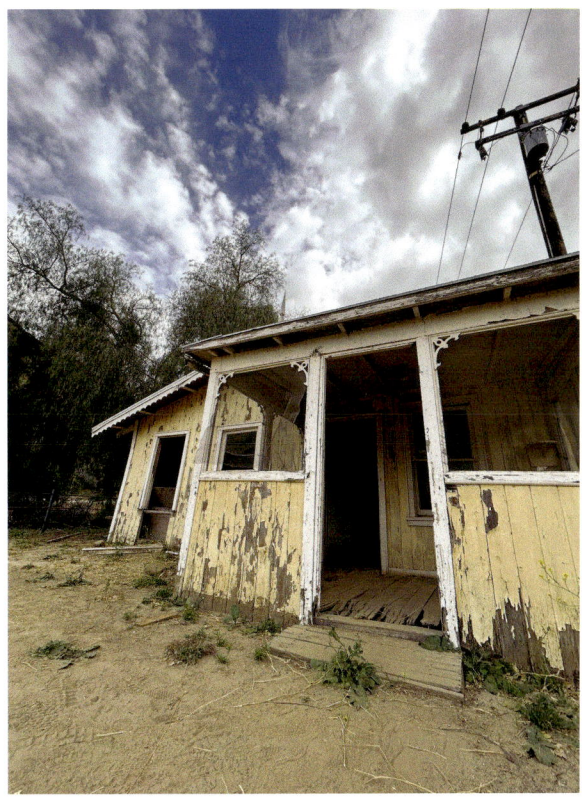

"Movie Facade House" was constructed at Mentryville in the late 1980s for the movie *Return to Green Acres* but has also been featured on other films, including *The Color Purple* and *The X-Files*.

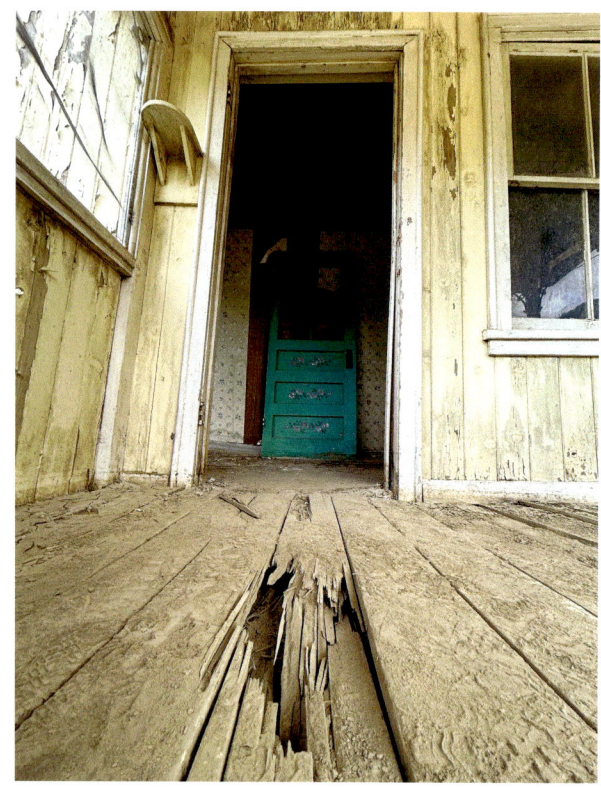

The beautiful turquois door of the Facade House has been removed and rests against the wall near the front entrance.

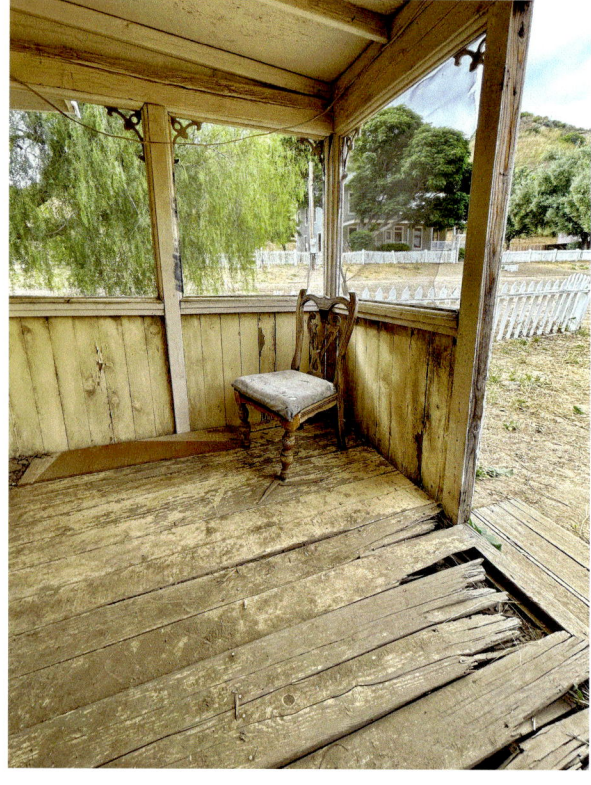

Another view of the front deck's ornate details, with the big house at Mentryville photobombing in the background.

Big Horn Mine

Deep within the San Gabriel Mountains, perched at 7,000 feet on Mount Baden-Powel, sits the skeleton of a structure that was once expected to be the location of California's largest gold mine, known as Big Horn Mine. The legend says that two men discovered the mine in 1895 while hunting big horn sheep in the area. With a total distance of 1,200 feet, this discovery was predicted to produce over $8 million in profit and employ 250 men. Unfortunately, this dream was over exaggerated, and within a few years, it was run by only three men and had only produce approximately $100,000 worth of gold.[2]

By 1936, it was decided that they would no longer excavate the Big Horn Mine, and the location was left abandoned. From forest fires to mudslides and earthquakes, this structure has sure seen its share of disasters, but the unbeatable canyon views are worth the rugged 3.7-mile roundtrip hike. The narrow trail over a rocky slope that once served as a wagon road is now the hiking trail which leads to a giant skeleton of a two-story mining facility that is now just an oasis for risk takers, graffiti artists, explorers, and photographers.

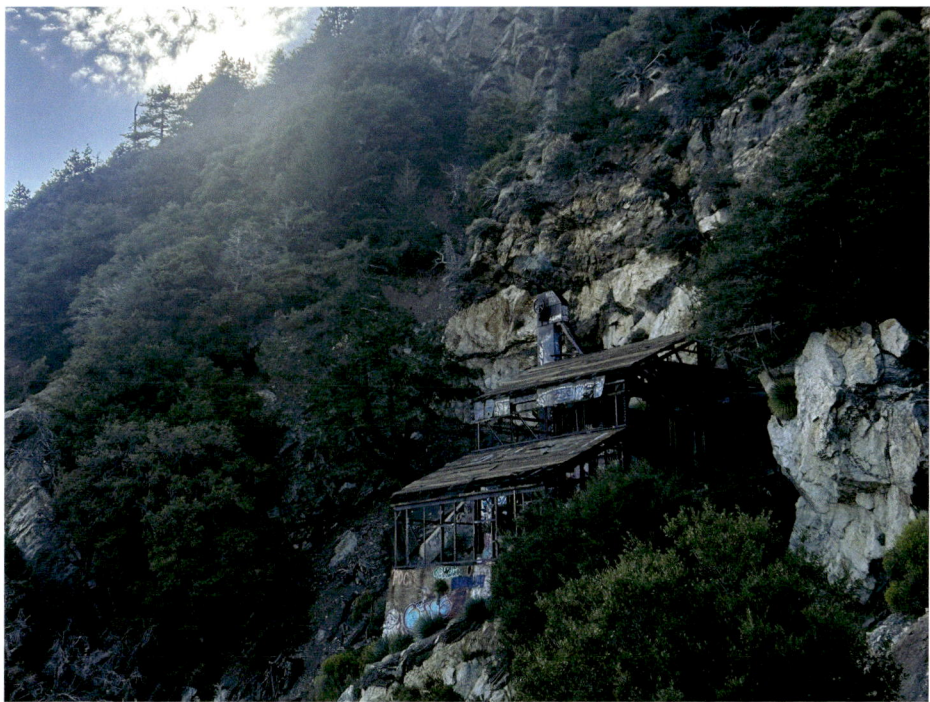

The first glimpse of Big Horn Mine as you turn the corner and witness the glory of what was once Los Angeles's biggest gold mine.

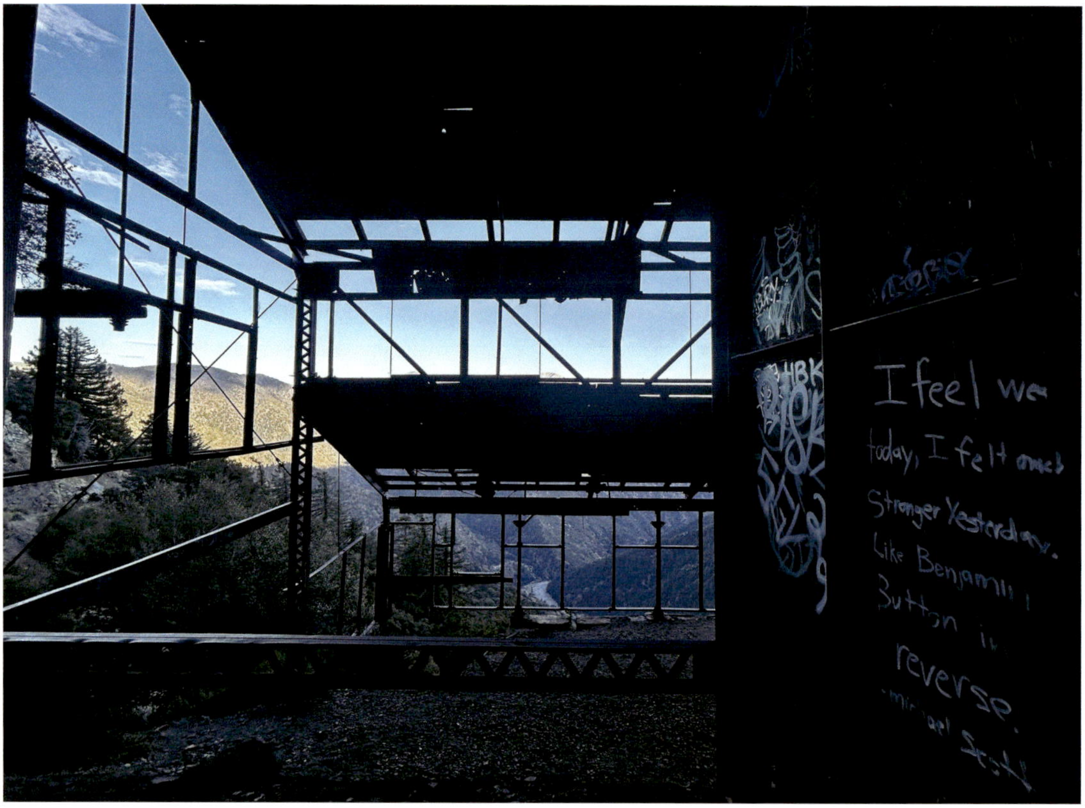

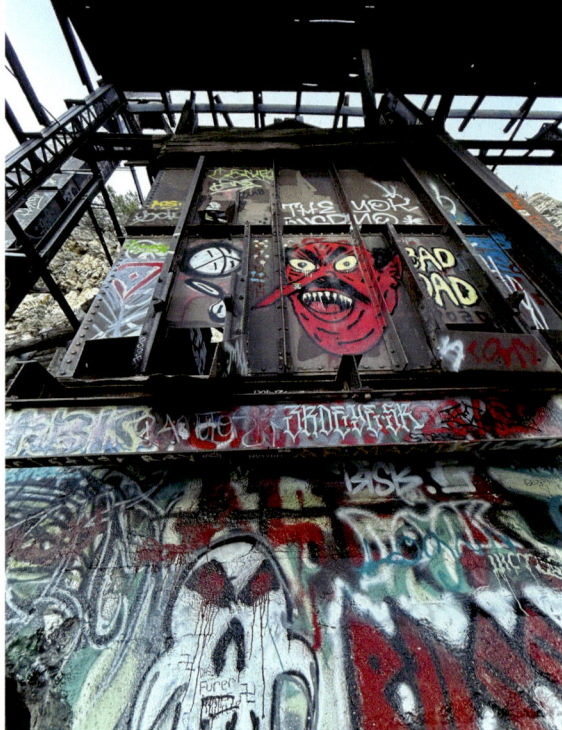

Above: A quote from the famous television show *The Office* painted on the side of a structural frame at Big Horn Mine.

Left: The inside of what is left of the old building that was once used to process all of the material that was coming out of the mine.

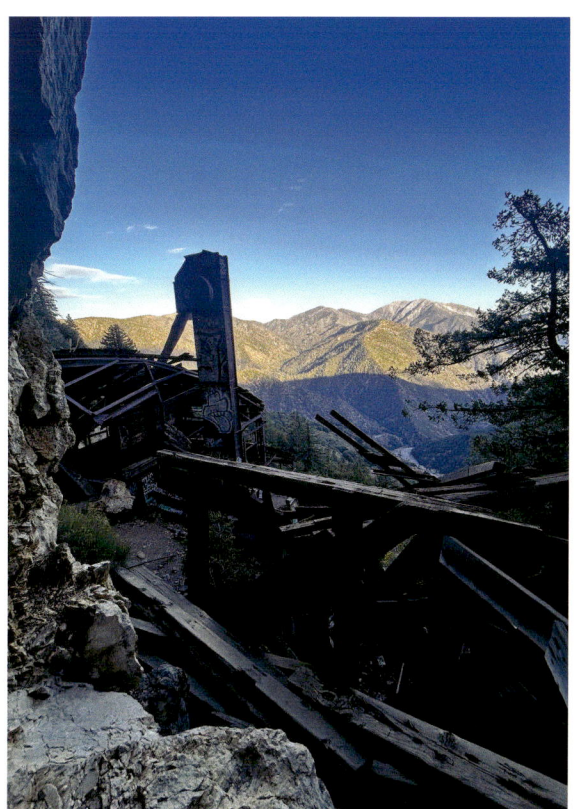

Looking out the entrance of the main mine at Big Horn Mine, you can see stunning views of Mount Baldy in the distance behind a collapsing minecart track.

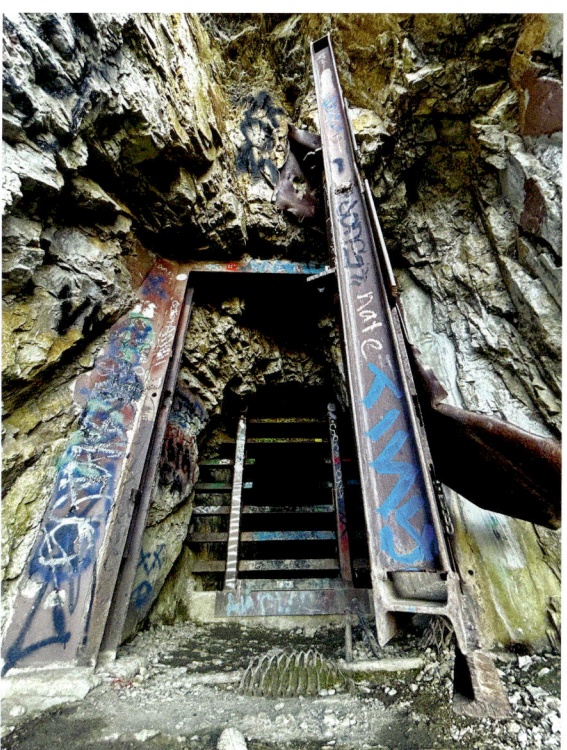

The entrance to the Big Horn mine, which leads to a 1,200-foot tunnel that once was California's largest gold mine.

4

THE HISTORIC HIGH DESERT

I spent half my life living in the High Desert, which is in northern L.A. County, where there was never much to do, so I spent a lot of time cruising around with friends, looking for new spots to explore. Yet every time I stumbled upon a new abandoned location, it amazed me that I had not discovered it sooner. No matter how sharp the eye is, I am constantly finding new ruins along highways I have traveled dozens of times.

Valyermo Ruins

Driving through California, you are bound to pass many abandoned structures, some of which are extremely hard to find history on, such as this quarry-faced ruin in Valyermo. This building style was exceedingly popular in California between 1910 and 1930 because it seemed to outlast most natural disasters. The remaining ruins give us an interesting glimpse of the popular architecture of the past. These rock homes seem to have proven themselves throughout history to outlast years of fires, earthquakes, and heavy rainstorms. Sitting right next door to the mysterious rock walls is this old wooden house, dilapidated, pigeon infested, and falling apart.

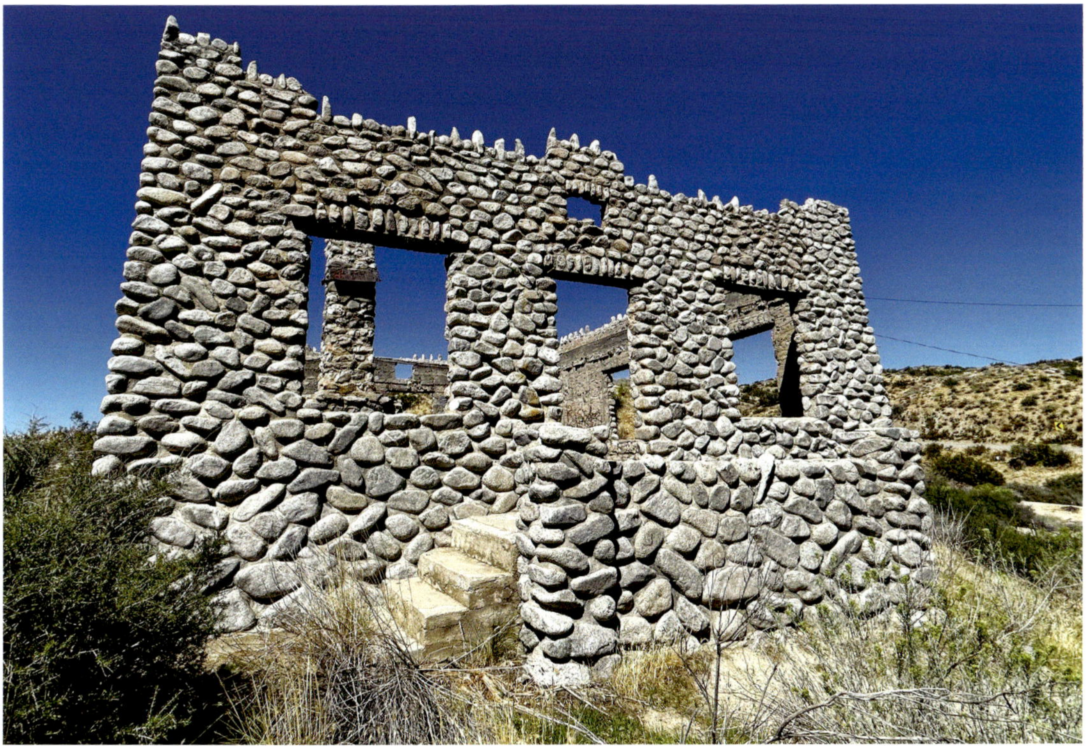

This stone structure sits perched upon a hill overlooking a very small valley in Valyermo. This style of building was immensely popular in the late 1800s and early 1900s.

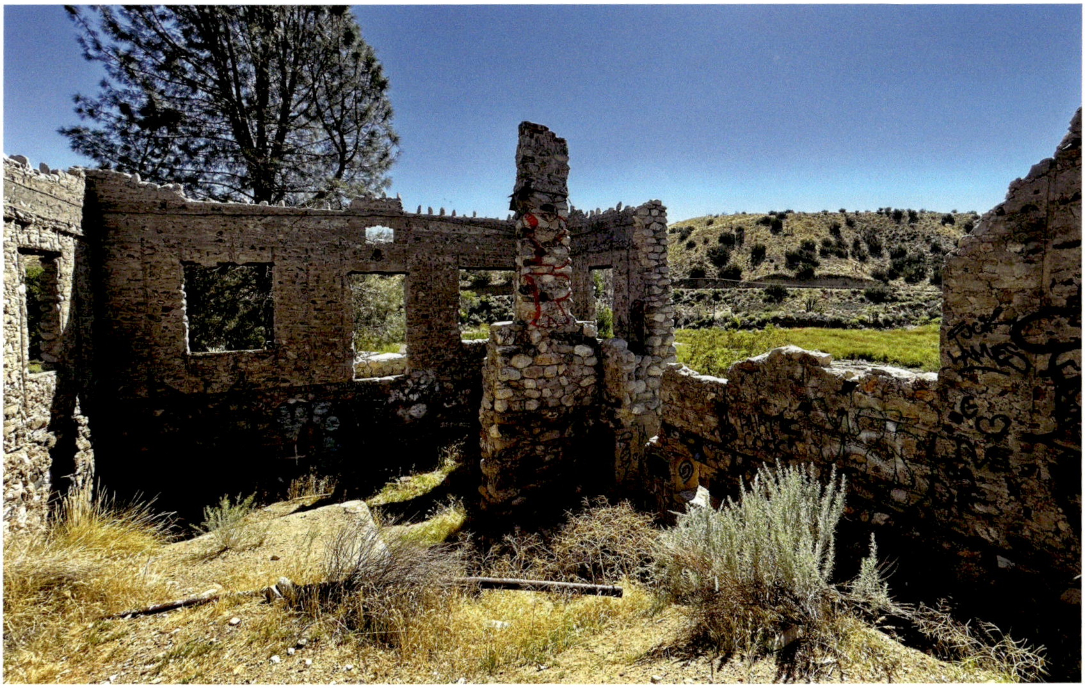

Now with only four walls and a fireplace remaining, the home is full of nothing but mystery and tumbleweeds.

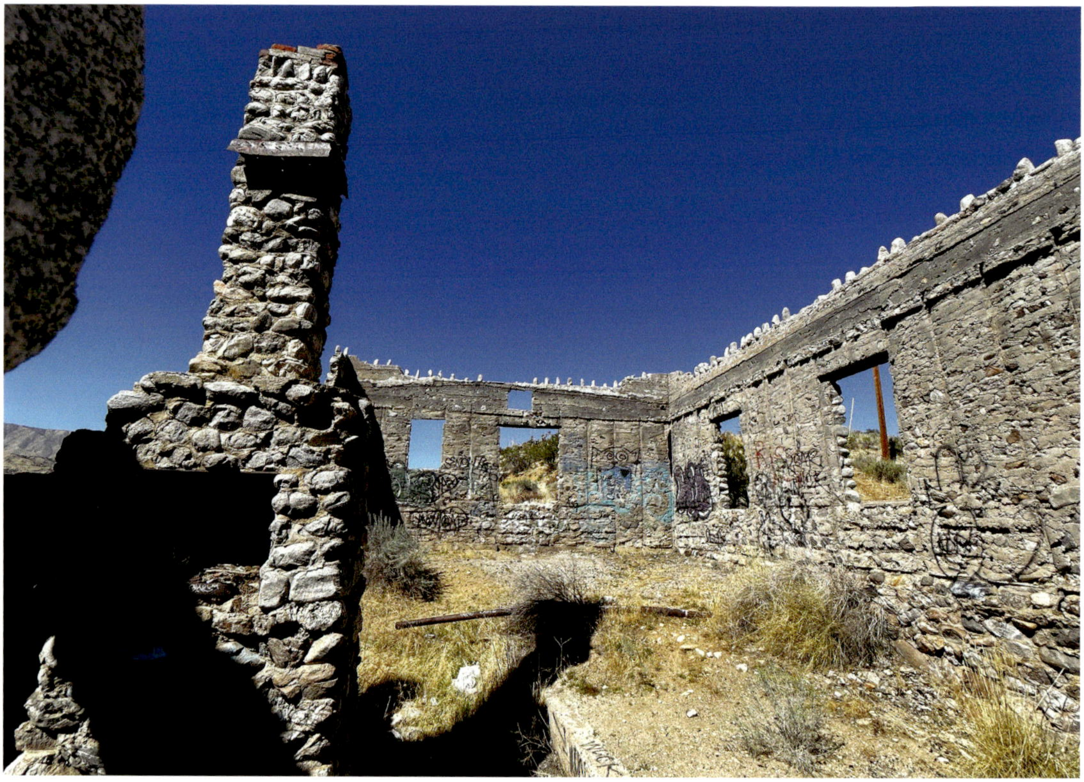

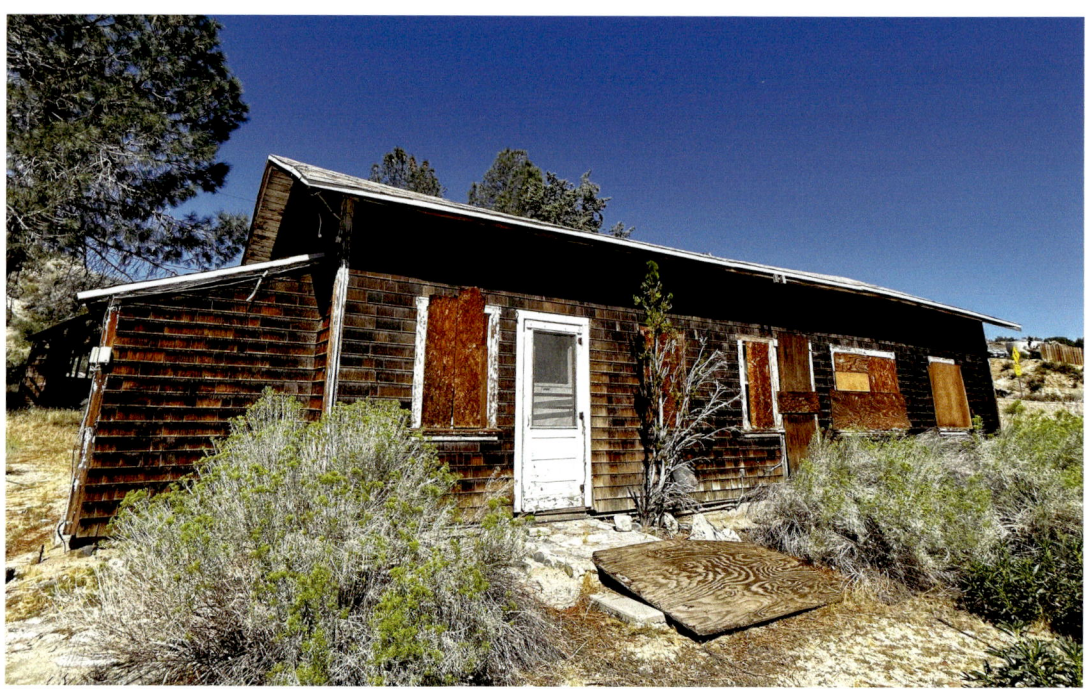

Judging by the height of the fireplace, this home most likely had a small basement at one time.

Right next door to the rock structure is a small, wooden, one-bedroom home that is slowly falling apart.

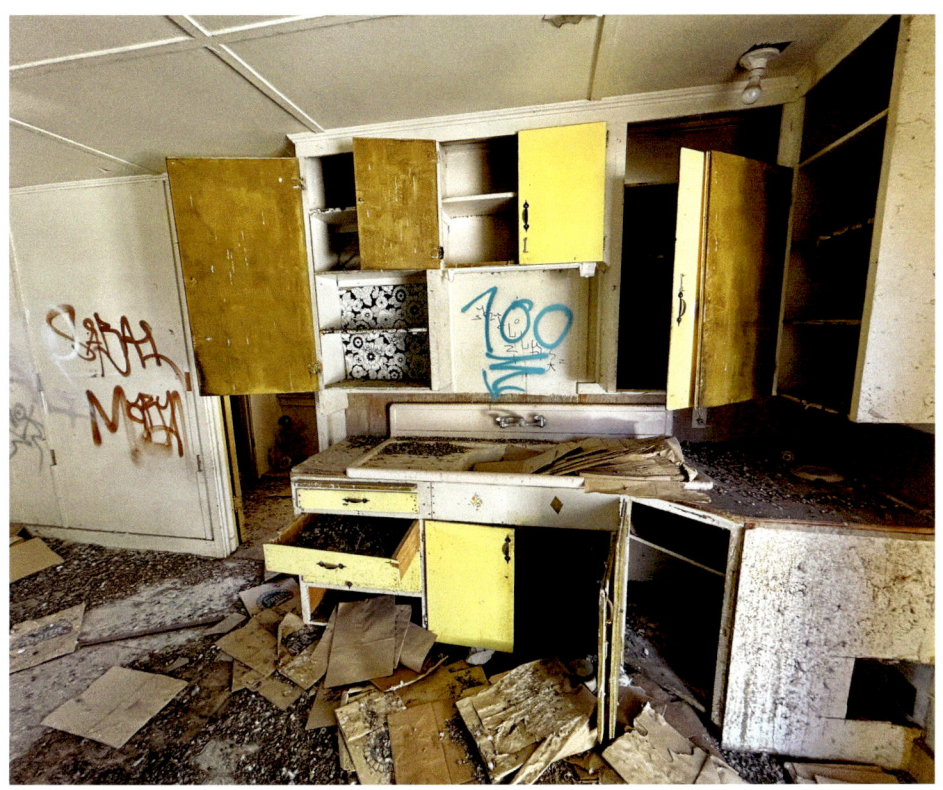

Yellow cupboards with black and white wallpaper lining the crumbling kitchen of a roadside home in Valyermo, California.

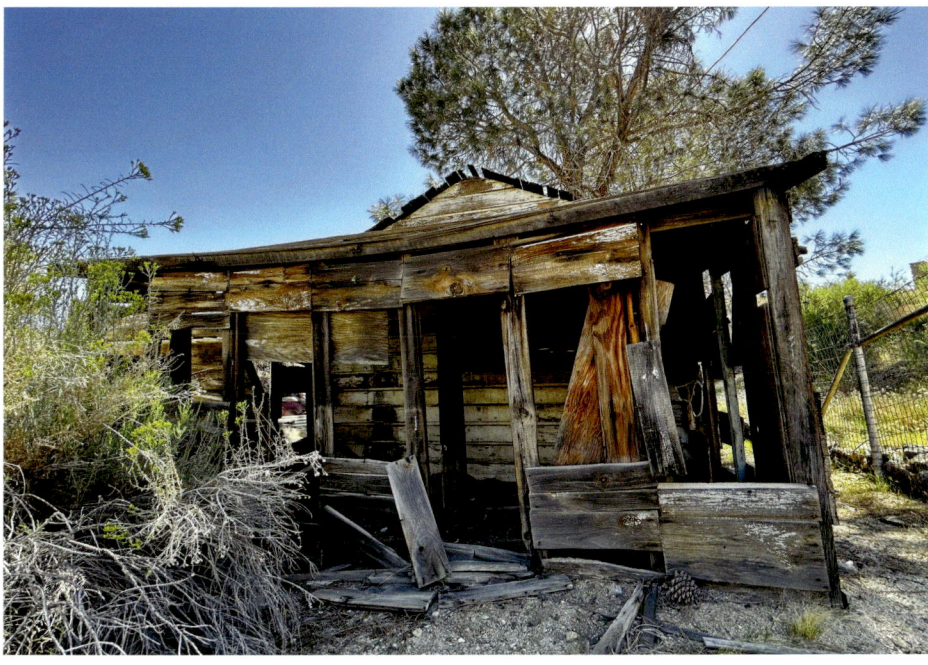

The wood home looks older from the outside, and the inside is now falling apart and nothing more than a home for the pigeons.

Canyon Ruins

The 14 Freeway is one of the most traveled freeways in L.A. County due to it being the only freeway connecting the High Desert to the San Fernando Valley. Hundreds of people travel this route every day heading to work or a quick getaway to the city, but most are unaware of the historic ruins that they are passing along the way. Like this *circa* 1800s stone structure, hidden in a small canyon, among what seems to be the ruins of a small ranch property. Although I am unable to find history on this place, it is very interesting because judging by the style of construction and a few artifacts left behind, I can tell that it is well over 100 years old and was most likely used by early settlers in the area.

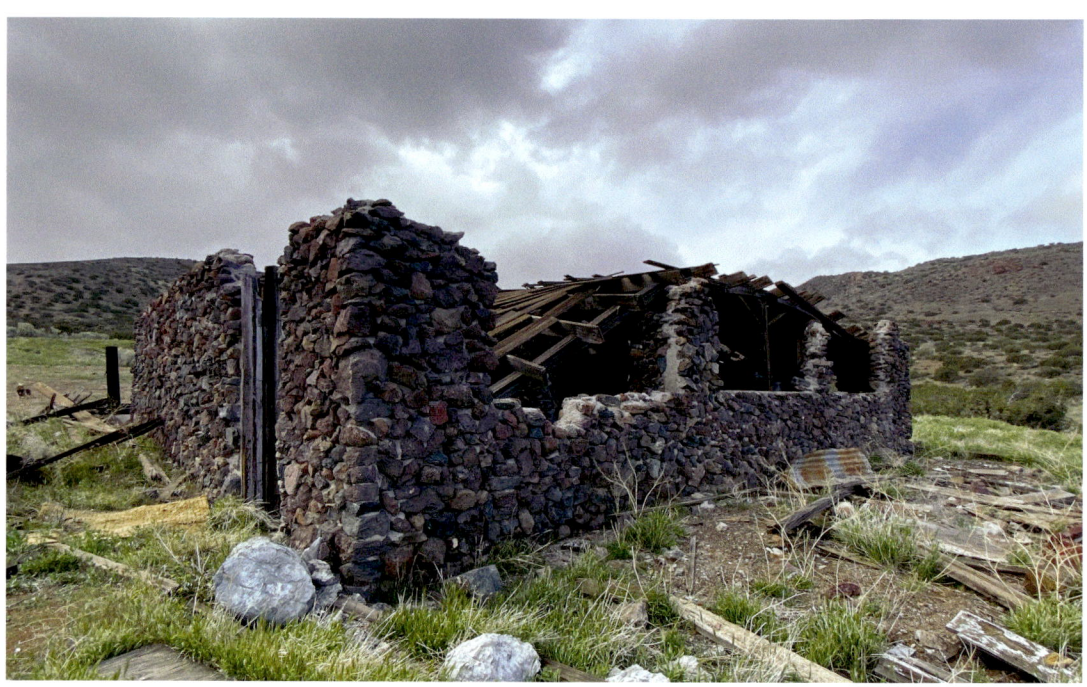

Built in the late 1880s and nestled along the hillside in Palmdale is what was one of the Antelope Valley's first settler's cottages.

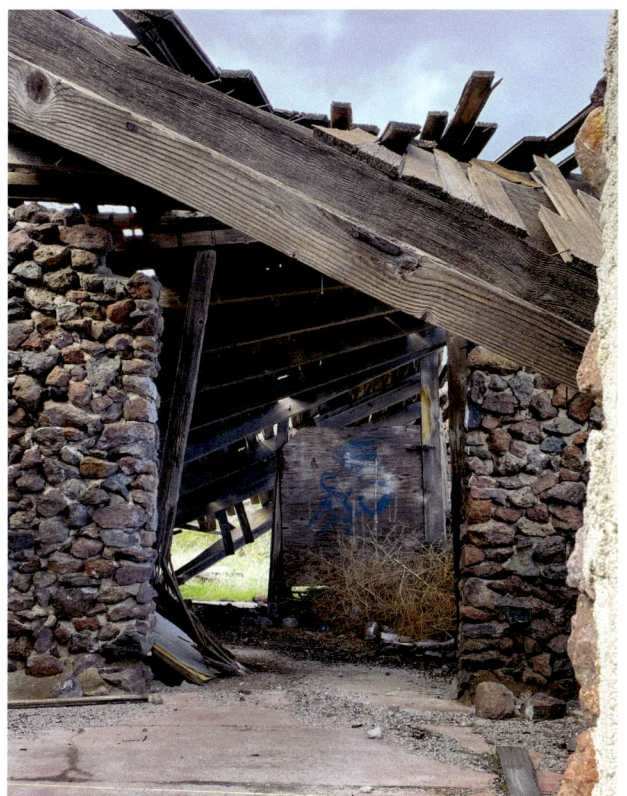

Right: Looking in from the entranceway of the old cottage, you can tell it once had very large windows to provide a full view of the small valley in front of the old home, but now the roof has collapsed and blocks anyone from enjoying its views any longer.

Below: Measured by Google Earth at about 300 feet long, I am assuming that this concrete wall once supported a barn or a large greenhouse.

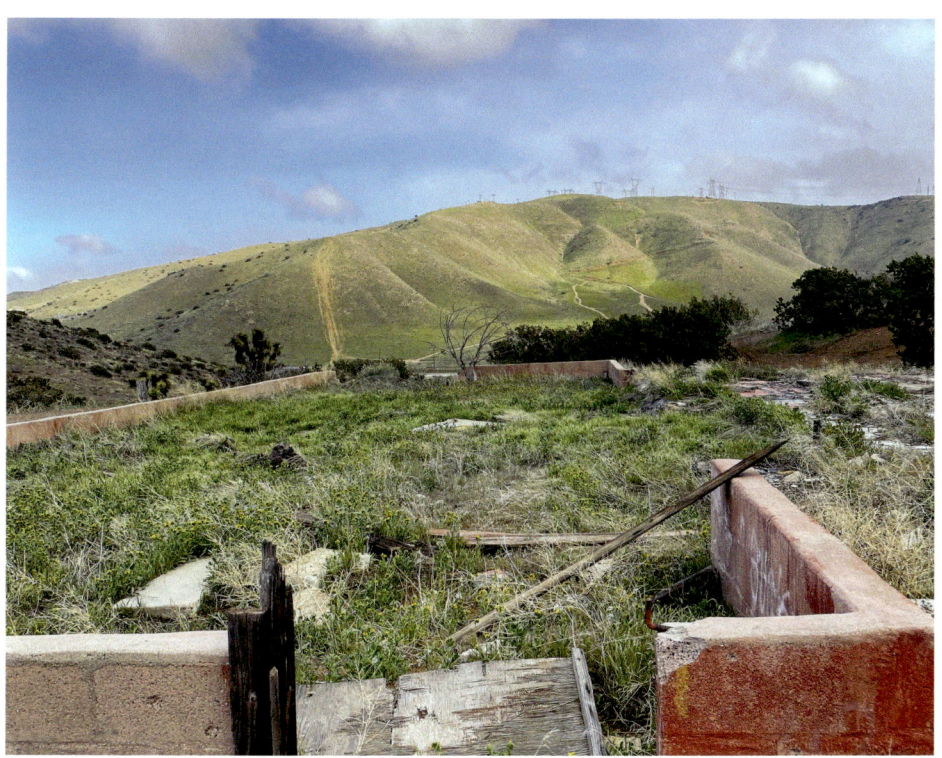

Lake Hughes' Church Camp

Tucked deep within the rolling hills of Lake Hughes is what seems to be the remnants of a church camp. It is noticeably clear that this property was engulfed by a devastating fire, leaving nothing but metal scraps, a few skeletons of old structures, and concrete basketball courts. Among the things still visible is a giant metal cross hanging upside down, presumably because of a fire that burnt the surrounding wood frame to a crisp. The cross, accompanied by the skeleton of an old school bus, and vast number of basketball courts, tells me that this was a place that people gathered to worship, although I was unable to find the exact history online.

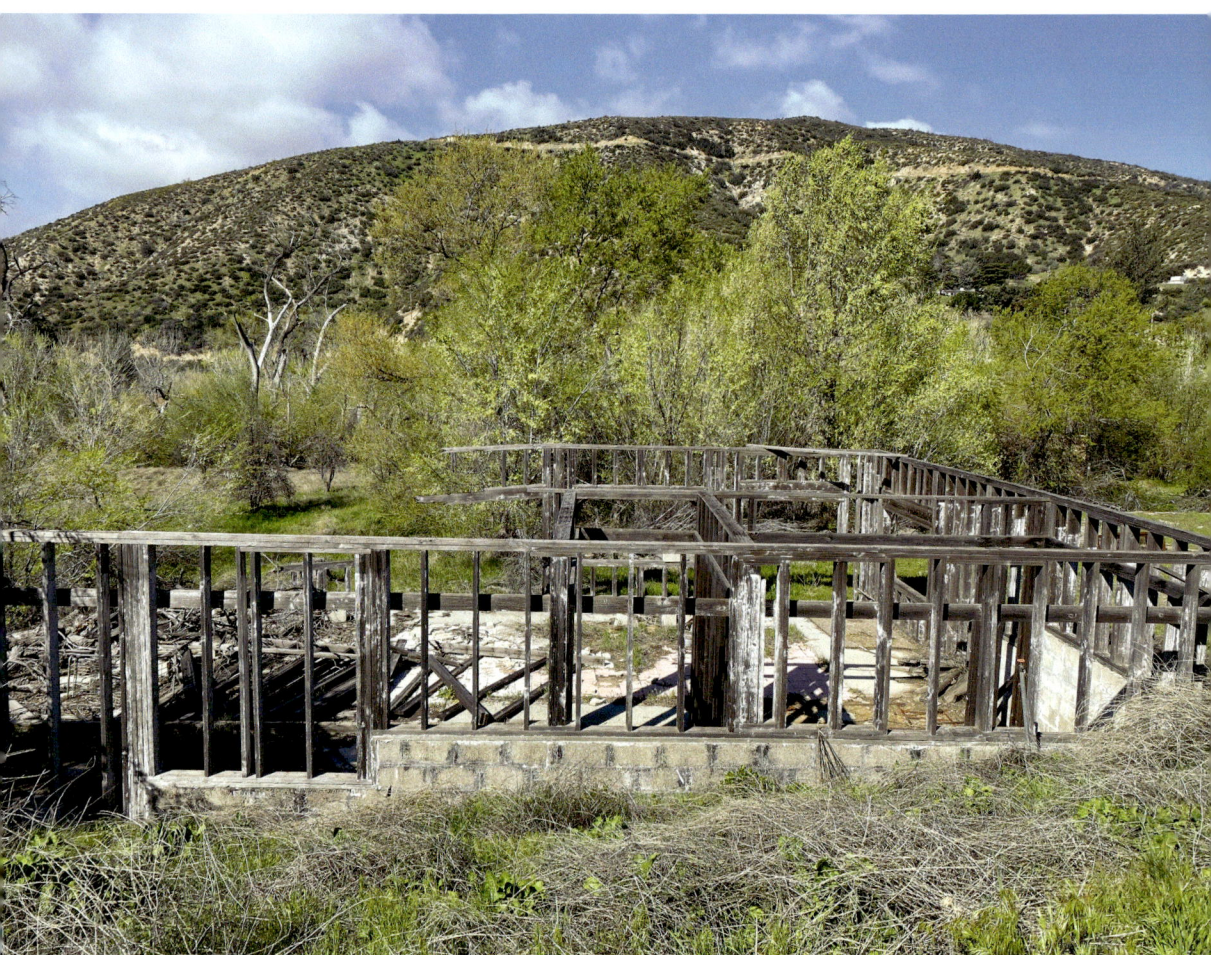

Wood beams are all that is left of the main structure on the property, what I believe was once a teenage church camp.

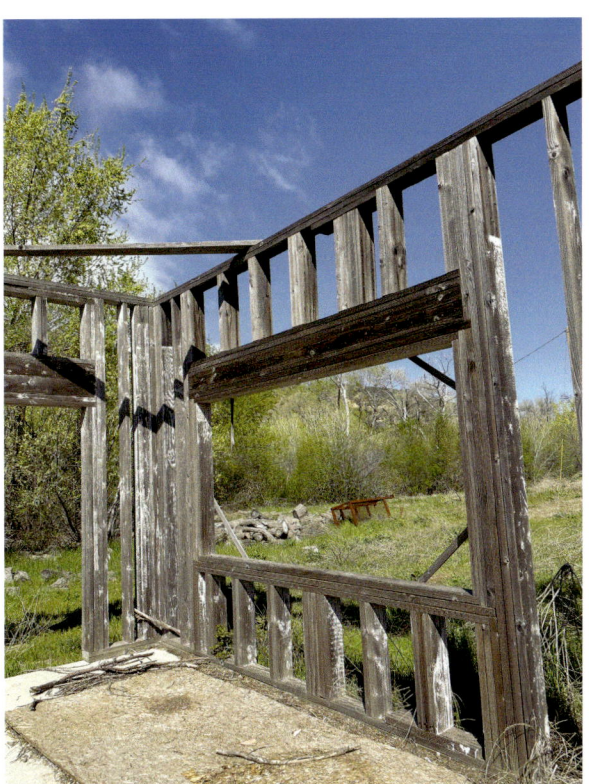

All that remains is the frame of a structure which somehow survived the several fires that ripped through this area.

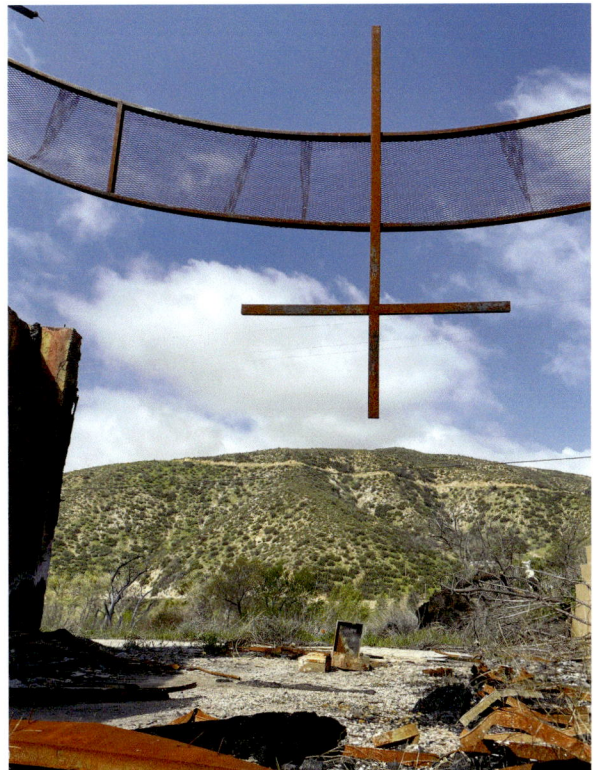

This cross now hangs upside down, but I assume that it was once an arched entrance way to a small chapel.

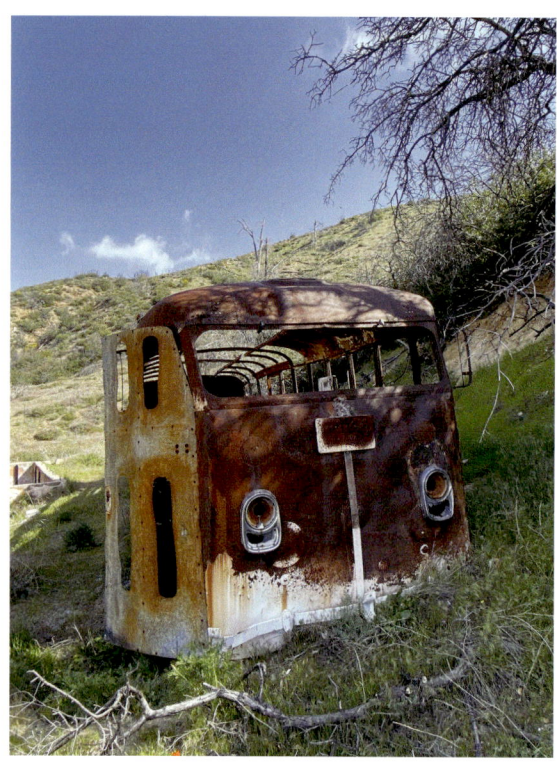

Left: This bus sits empty and rusted, leaving us to wonder about all the fun trips that may have once taken place via this 1950s-style bus.

Below: The view through the front window makes this spot a perfect last resting spot for this old bus.

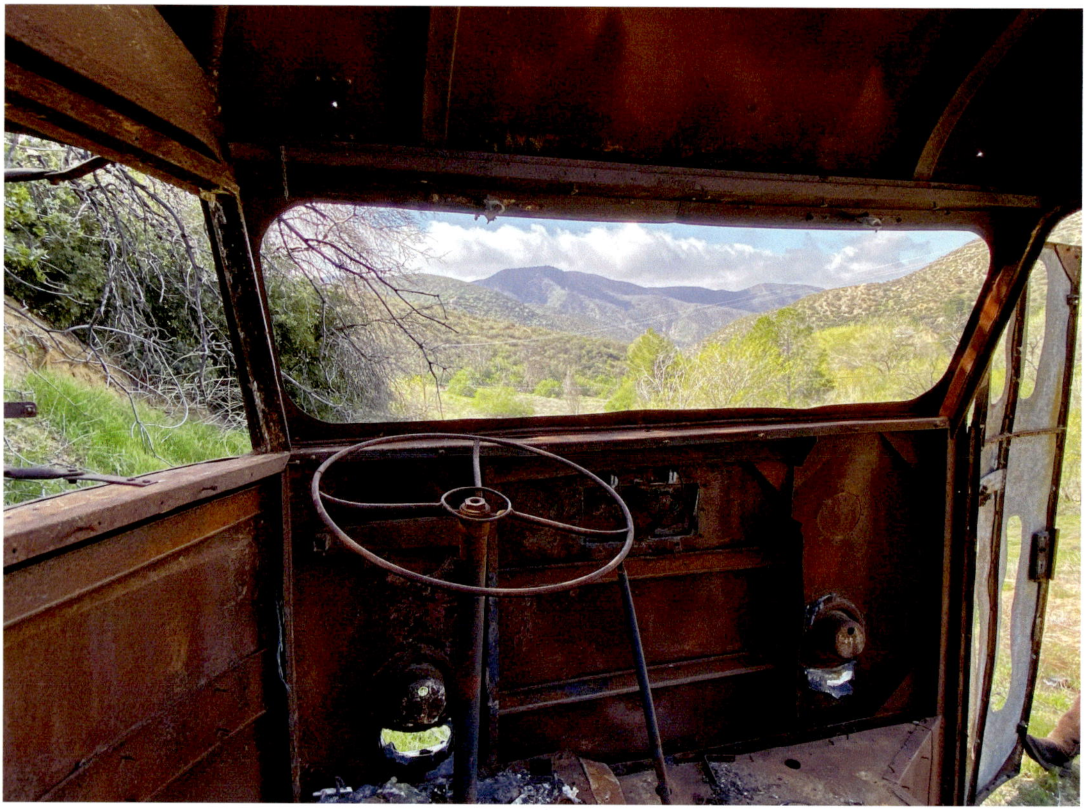

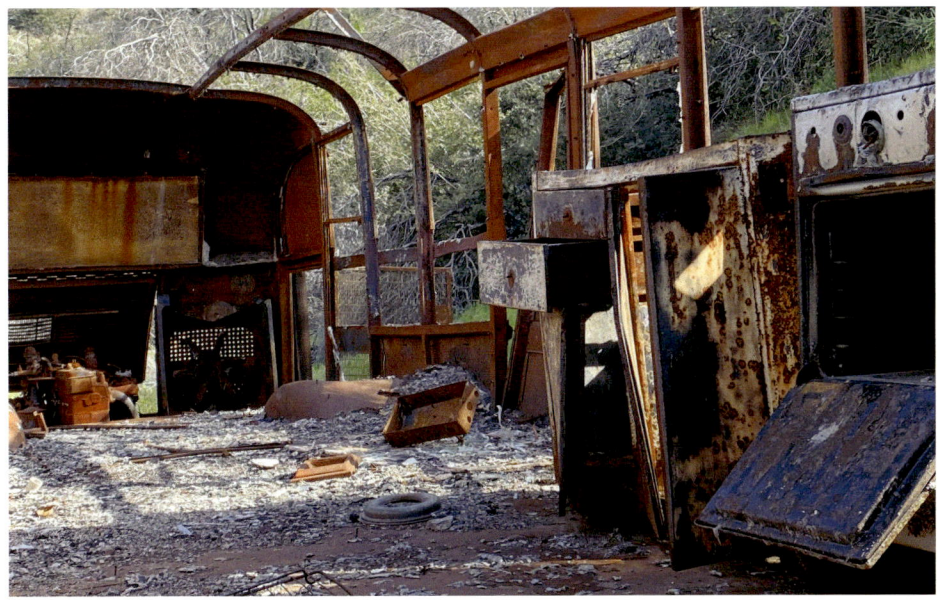

The inside of the bus surprisingly still had a solid floor and several ovens inside, suggesting that this was most likely transformed into a living quarter at one time.

Philips Ranch

One place that really catches my eye has an interesting but uncertain history: Philips Ranch. The land was originally granted to a man named Ben Hikin in 1914, but in 1924, he was forced out to make room for the Saint Francis Dam. So, the land then remained submerged for the next decade, until the dam collapsed and damaged nearly everything in its path. The ranch was not rebuilt until 1952 when the land was acquired by the Philips family.

They built a gorgeous, three-bed, three-bath ranch-style home and soon began construction of a restaurant and extravagant pool suitable for their dream of building a resort hotel. Eventually, the small resort became quite popular and even offered fun activities such as horseback riding, swimming, an aviary, and a shooting range.[1] Rumor has it that it may have once been a brothel, but that story could not be confirmed.

Many people report having wonderful memories of this place, and it is uncertain what led to the beloved ranch being left vacant for so long, but there is some record of several different foreclosures taking place on the property. It seems no one was able to keep this property afloat, and in 2002, the Copper fire destroyed the remaining structures. All that remains are 20-foot cement walls of what was once the main building, winding pathways with small bridges hinting at some type of creek running through the property, an empty but elaborate swimming pool, and the echoes of laughter of the good times once spent at Philips Ranch.

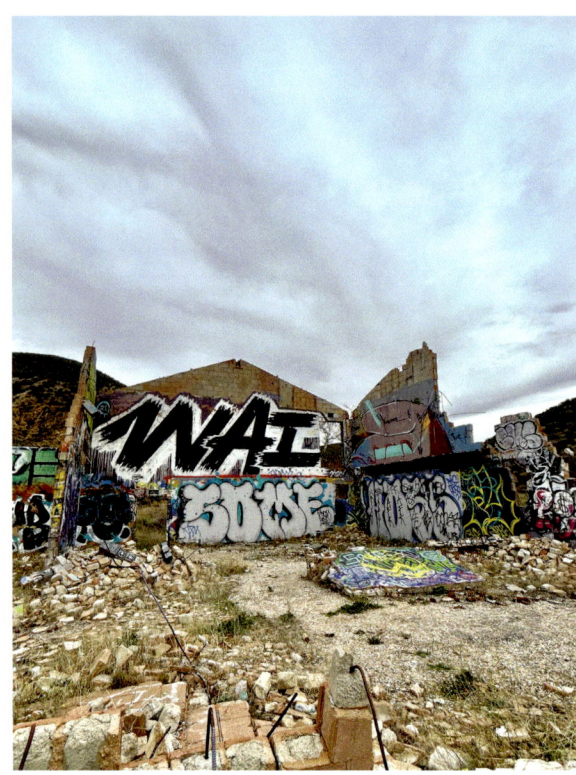

This is all that is left of the main structure on Philips Ranch, which was believed to once serve as a hotel, restaurant, bar, and possibly even a brothel.

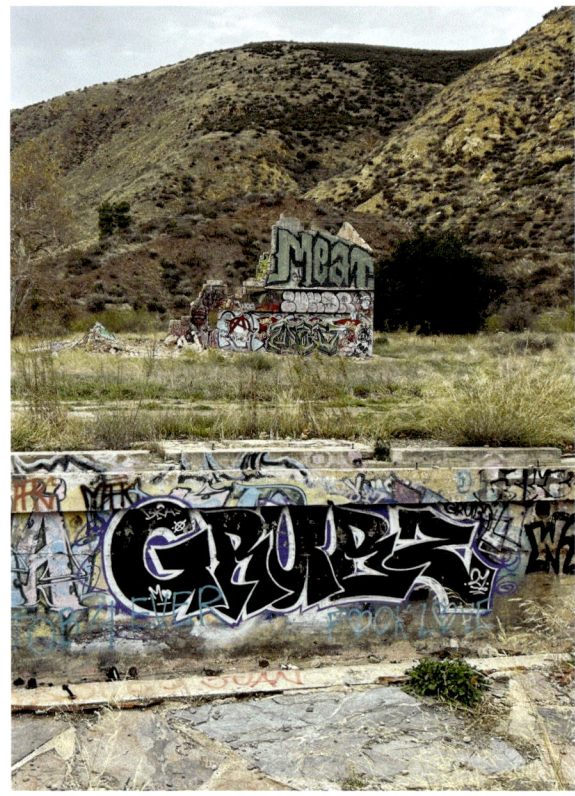

If you were hanging out by the pool looking back towards San Fransquito Rd, this would be your view, although I am sure it was once much more beautiful and livelier.

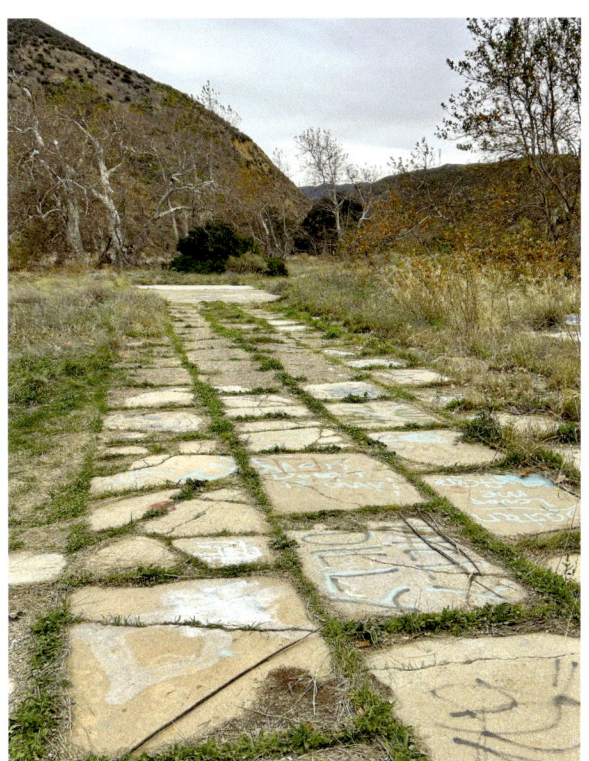

The walkway leading up to a very inviting and fun ranch that was once designed to not only be a family's ranch but also had plans of becoming a booming resort.

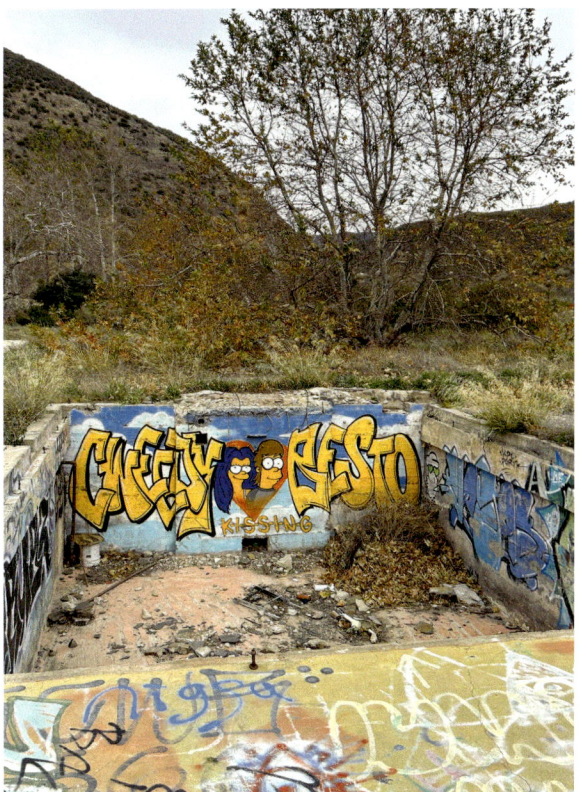

A concrete pit that I think could have been used as some type of storage or something.

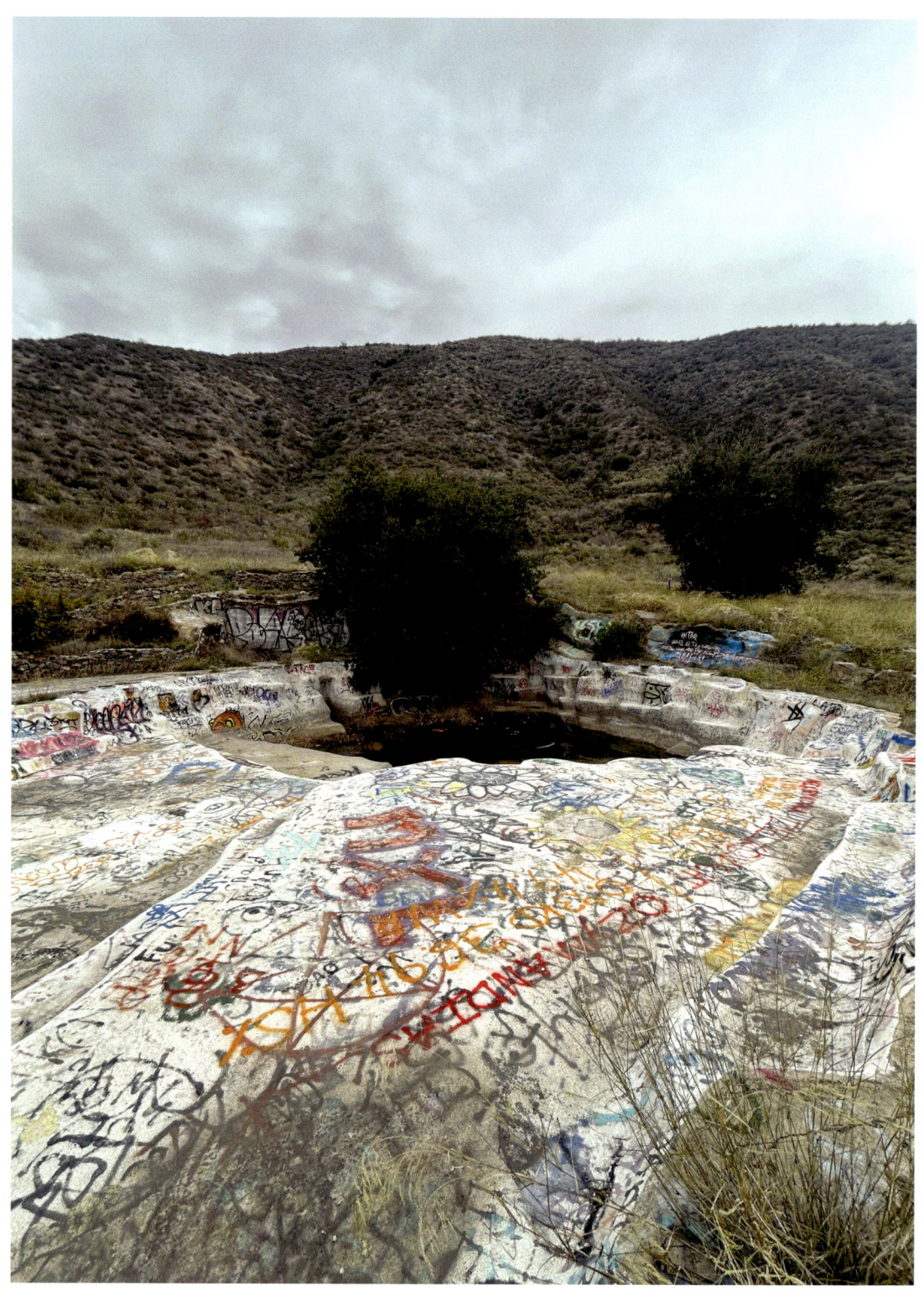

The pool at Philips Ranch was huge, with cascading depths of a waterfall, water slide, and cave. What was once a beautiful oasis is now just a breeding ground for mosquitos.

5

VACANT MANSIONS OF L.A. COUNTY

E very abandoned place has its own story, whether it is pleasant, or dark, is often unknown, but every now and then the story is so tragic and heart breaking that it remains in the minds of the community and homeowners forever. With property values being so high in L.A. County, it is extremely rare for any property to be vacant for more than a few years, and when it is, it makes us wonder what happened to keep these beautiful properties from being revamped. Sometimes it may be as simple as being a registered historic landmark with extensive restoration costs, or worse, a messy divorce, or gruesome murder.

Mysterious Mansion

A mysterious mansion in Los Angeles sits right smack dab on one of the most prestigious beaches in all of California, yet it has been abandoned by its owner for over twenty years. The home was bought in 1993 by Gordan Getty, and later sold to his mistress, Cynthia Beck, after scandal broke out about their affair and three illegitimate children. Several years later, the neglected home rapidly began to decay to the elements. Extremely dilapidated and seemingly forgotten about, it is said that property taxes are still being paid, and urban explorers in the past even found that the power was still on inside of the house. Now the home is much less accessible, and it is believed to have been boarded up by neighbors to prevent the ruckus that the property was bringing to the area. Its architecture and views are still gorgeous despite the despair, and as I sit on the marble porch, I can't help but think about the heartbreak that must be tied to the memories in this home.

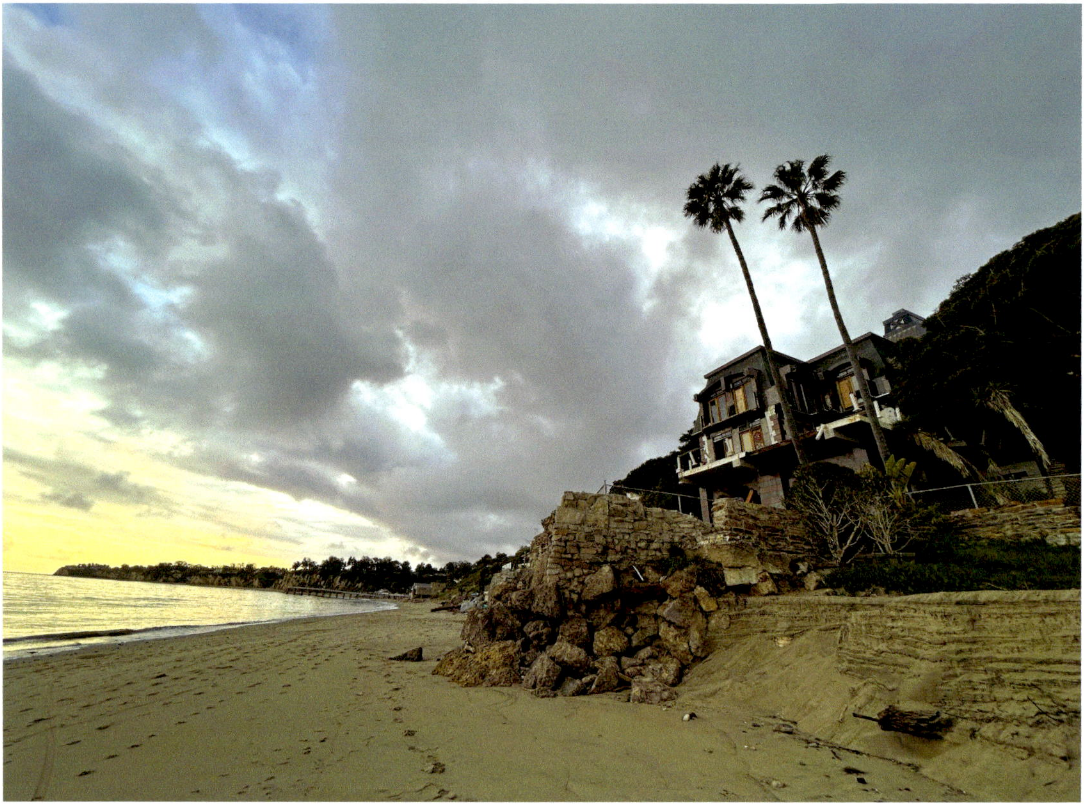

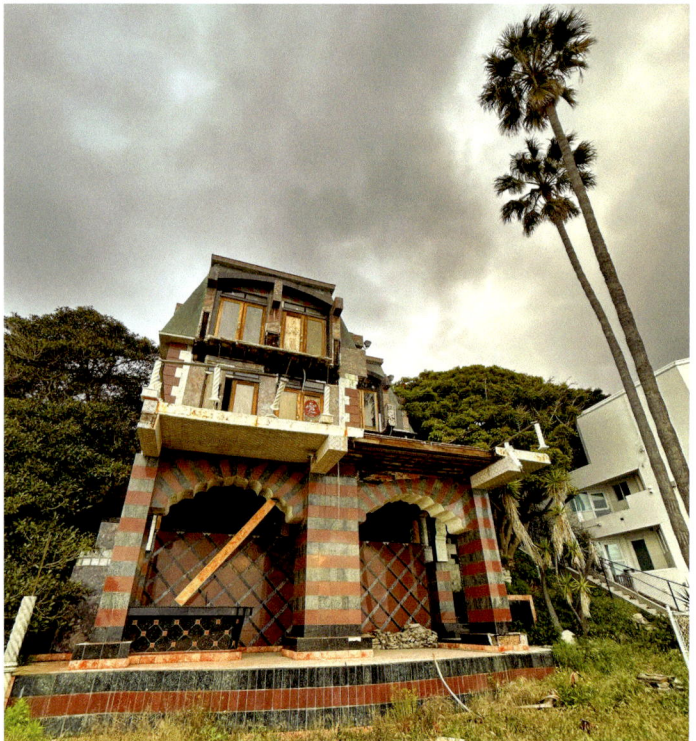

Above: The amazing ocean-front property sits neglected and decaying on one of the most beautiful and expensive beaches in the United States.

Left: The intricate details of this home are incredible and show that someone put a lot of thought into its design, yet they let it slowly fall away into the sea.

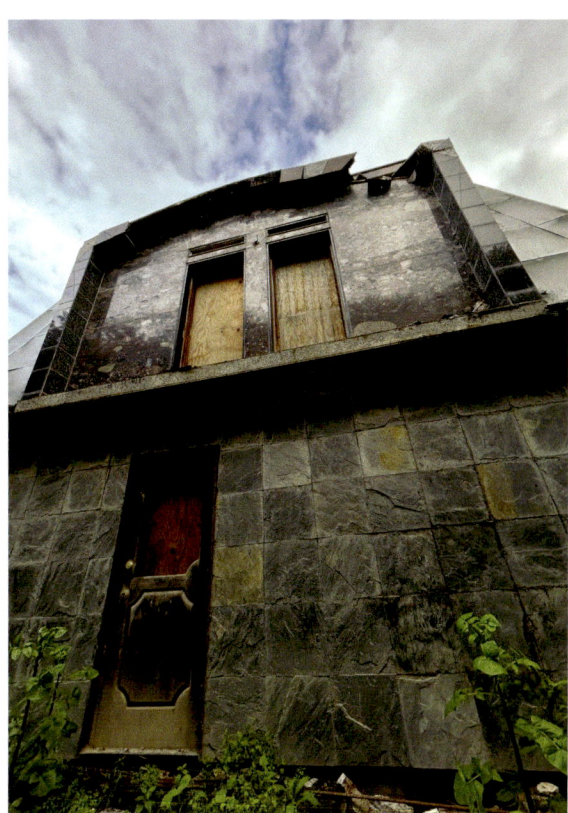

The home is covered in dark shades of marble, including grey, green, red, and traditional black and white.

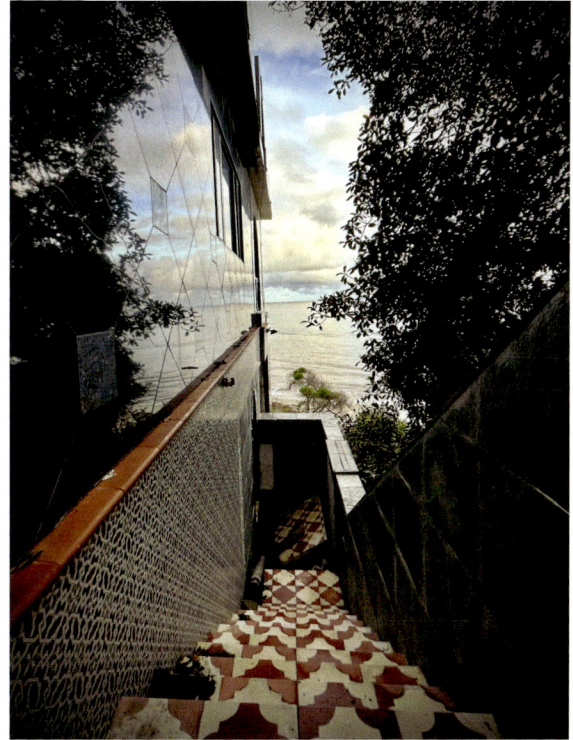

Each wall, door, staircase, deck, and path includes patterns, carvings, and art, giving us a glimpse of the beautiful artwork that was put into this mansion's construction.

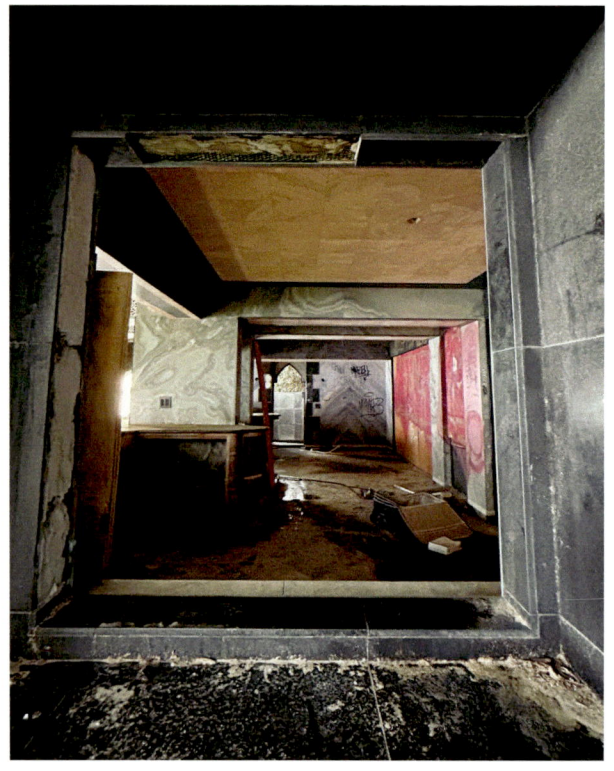

The view from a porch window looking into a space that once was used to host elaborate parties and relaxing barbeques.

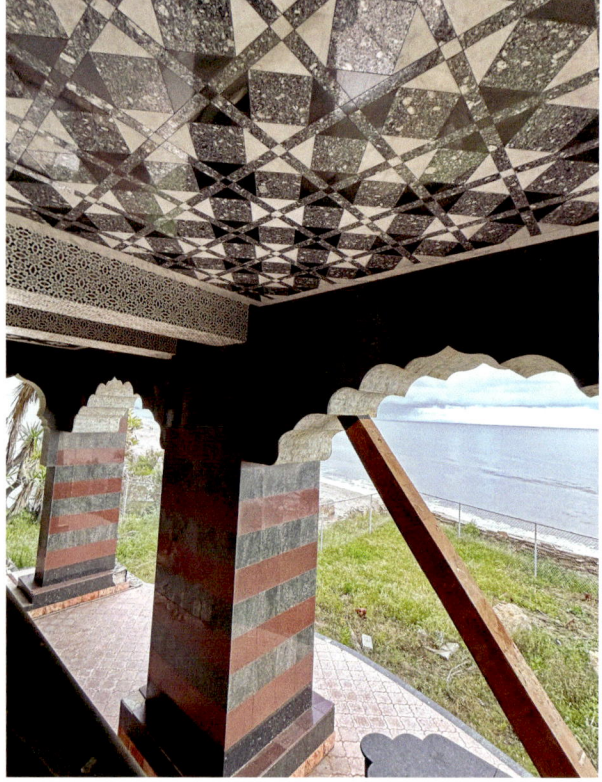

Huge marble tiles cover the exterior of the home from floor to ceiling, adding to the amazing view from this patio space.

Tom Morales Square

A famous historic neighborhood known as Tom Morales Square has the highest concentration of Victorian-style residences in L.A. County. Luckily, most of the historic mansions are occupied and have been beautifully restored, but there are a few that sit, lonely, waiting to be brought back to life. Many dating back to the early 1900s and earlier, the traditional Victorian architecture is hard to find in Los Angeles, but Lincoln Heights is a neighborhood where you can still catch a glimpse of the glorious historic L.A. homes. These properties are a perfect example of historic places waiting for the proper funding to bring them back to life again.

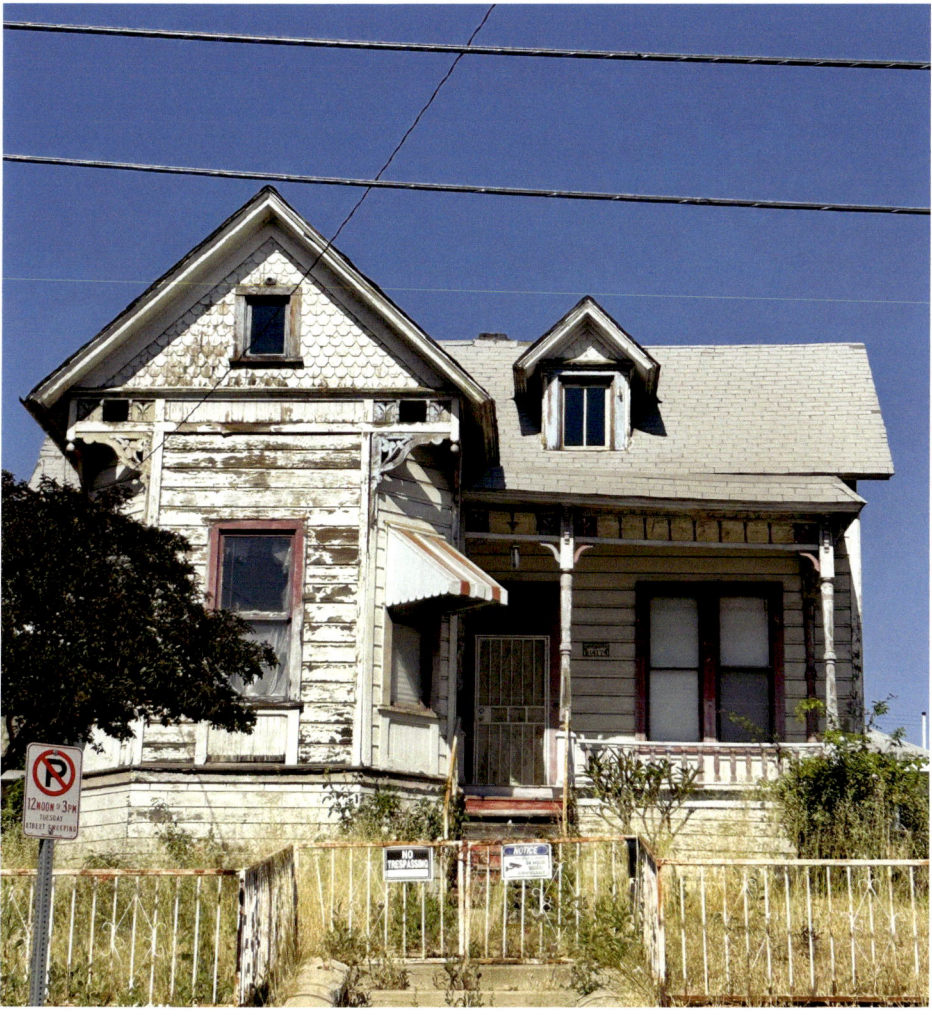

This historic, five-bedroom Victorian-style home was built in 1882 and last sold in 2017, but it has not been renovated since 1897 so it is unsure what the property owners plan to do with it.

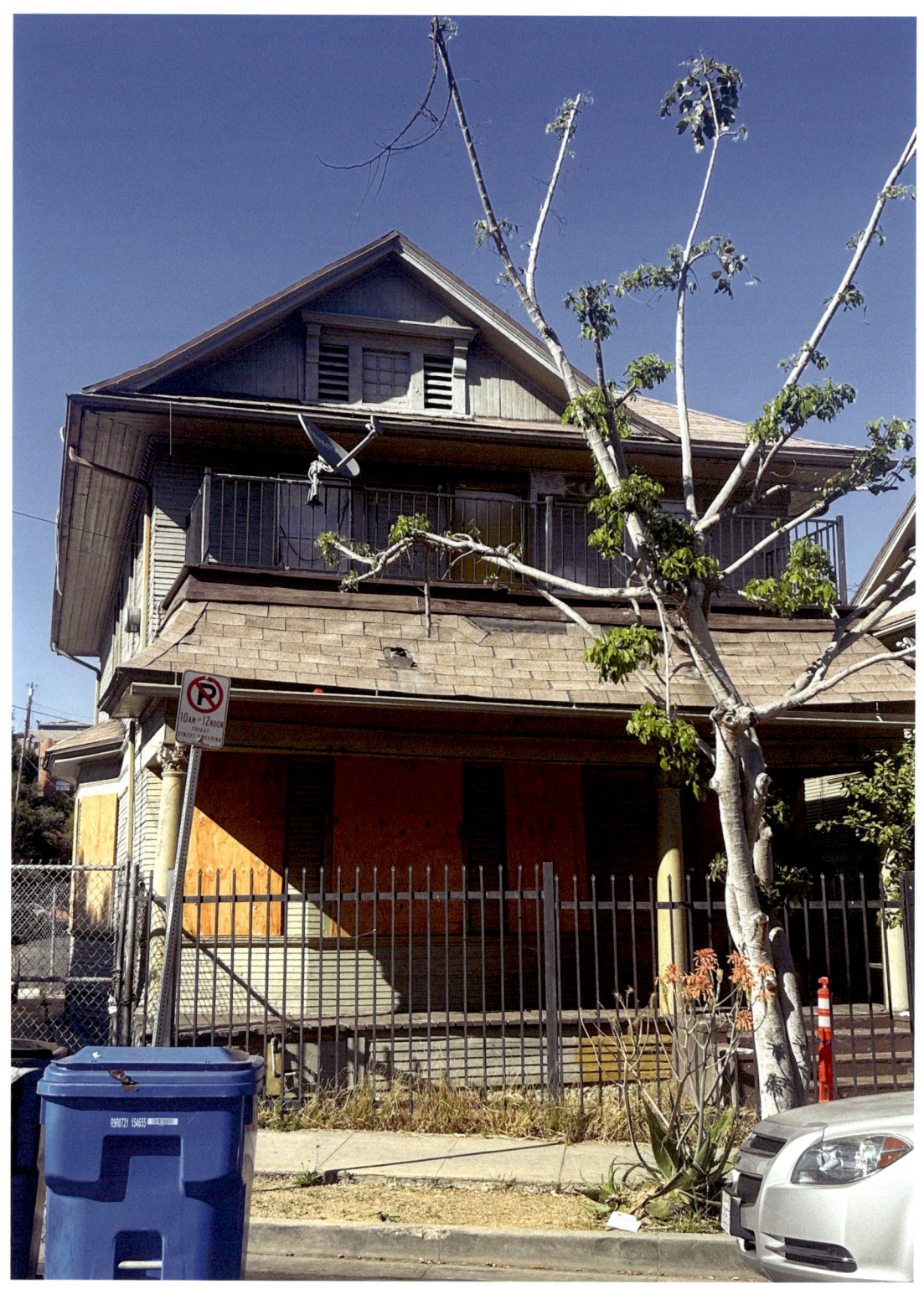

This historic home in Lincon Heights looks as if it is abandoned since its doors and windows are boarded up but when you look closer, you can see that it is currently housing a family on the top floor.

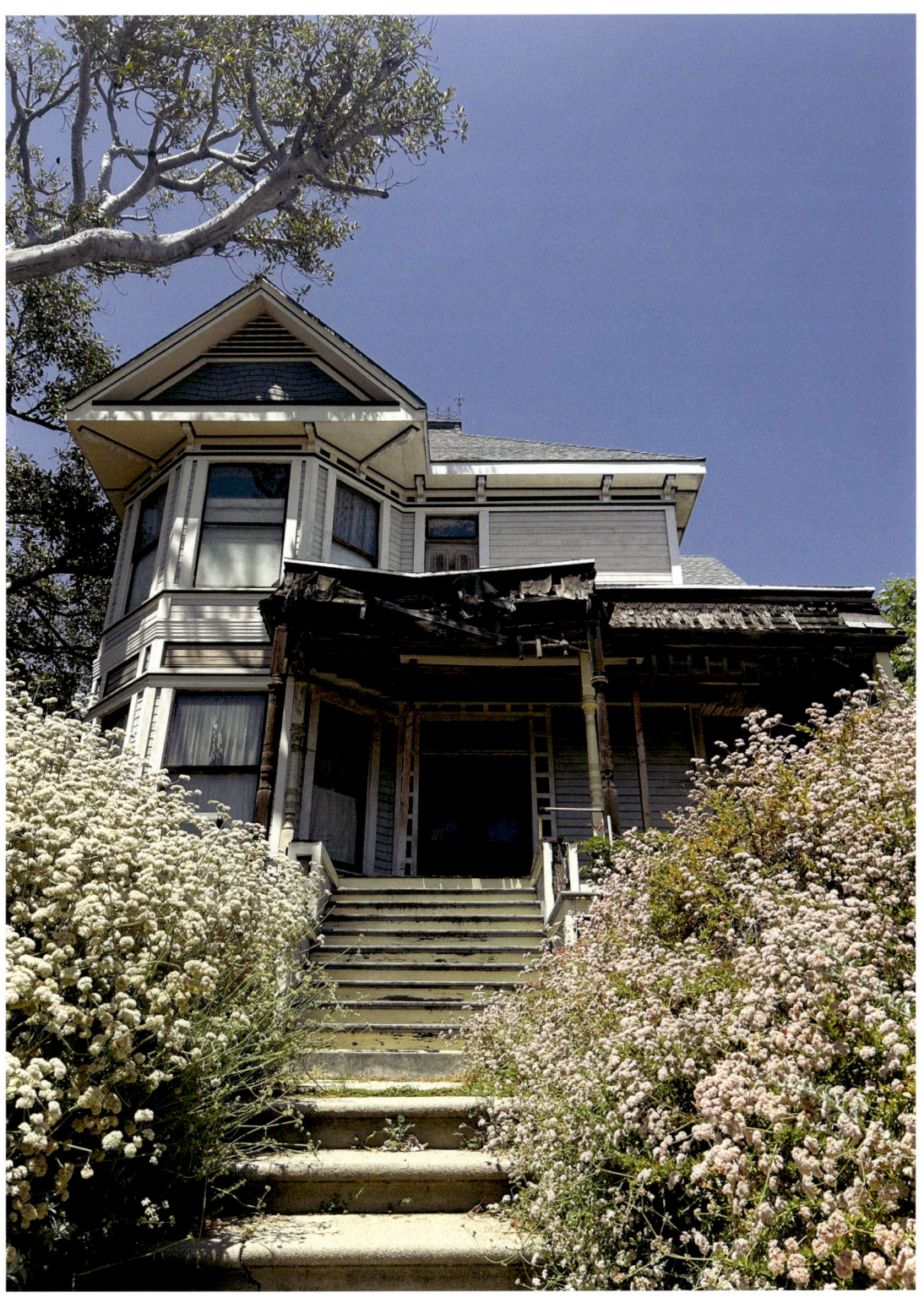

This home was made famous for the legendary 1983 music video, "Thriller." Although the home was purchased many years ago, it still has had no renovations preformed on the outside

West Adams

Another historic neighborhood in Los Angeles is West Adams. Most of its residences were built between 1880 and 1900, and it is one of the largest historic neighborhoods in L.A. County. It was slowly deteriorating, but now most of the homes have been restored and it is a gorgeous neighborhood once again. It is very uncommon to see a vacant and unrestored home in this area, but there is one that sticks out like a sore thumb. It was built in 1908, next door to the famous South Seas Home, which has very similar architecture. Coincidently, the two homes sat vacant together for decades, but one has now been beautifully restored and currently serves as a community center. Hopefully the community center continues to thrive and maybe one day they can expand to save the neighboring house as well.

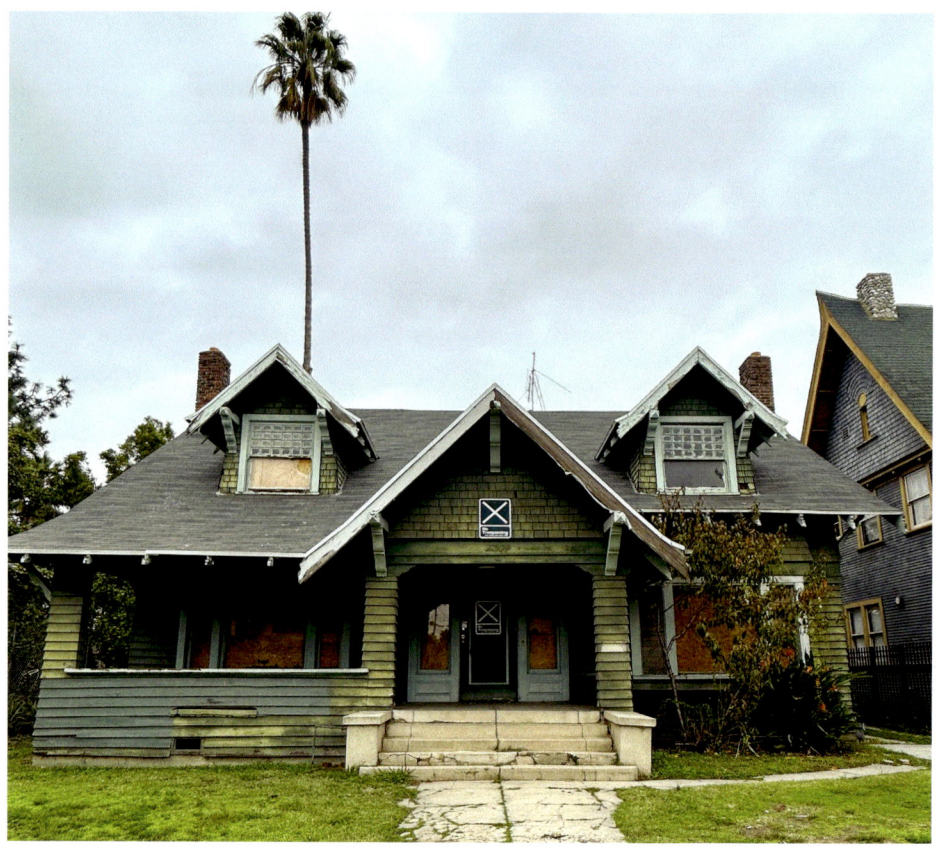

Although little history can be found on this 1908 Victorian-style home in West Adams's historic district, its architecture is so unique and beautiful that it is only a matter of time until a lucky investor decides to take on the project of its restoration.

Peabody Werden House

The Peabody Werden House was built in 1895 in a neighborhood called Boyle Heights, in East Los Angeles. Although there was not much history that I found about the house, I do know it is most famous for its Queen Anne architecture, a style that was once quite common for the area. The home was named after Josiah Peabody, a journalist for the *Los Angeles Times*, and a bookkeeper from South Refining Company named William Werden.[1] The historic home has been abandoned for decades, and in 2016, it was reinforced for protection and then moved across the street to make space for affordable housing units. Many plans are underway for the house, focusing on an office space for the Boyle Heights Historic Society, as well as a community meeting center, space to hold wellness classes, and even a community garden. Fifty affordable housing units are under construction at the site where the home was originally built, along with another sixty units on the vacant lot next to the home's new location.

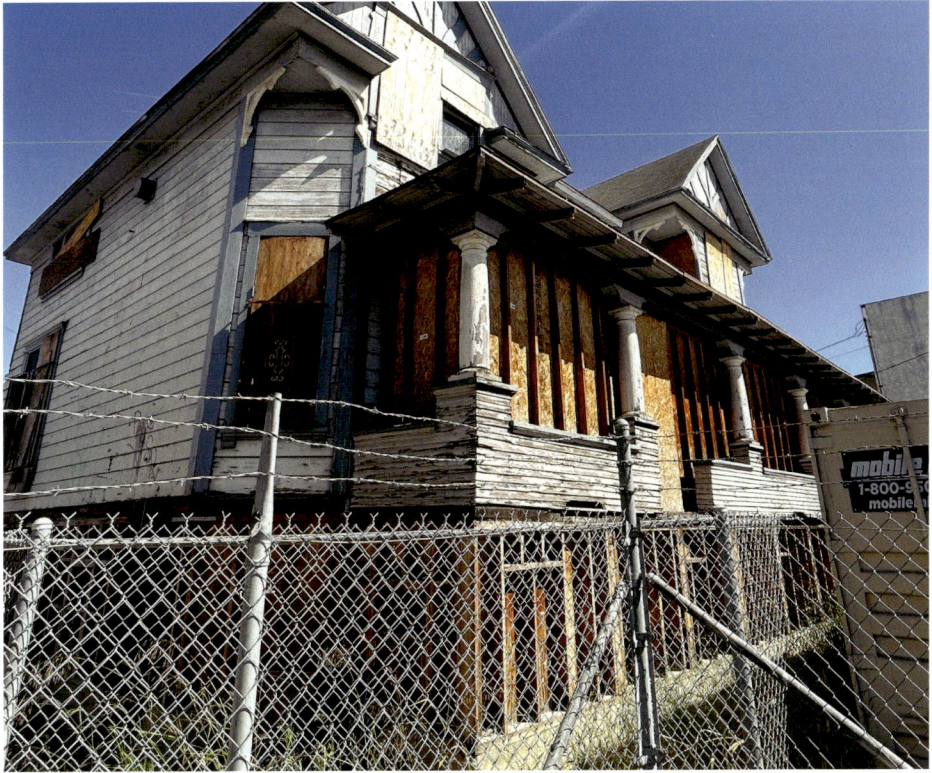

Peabody-Werden House is a registered historic landmark that has been relocated to its current spot to save it from demolition.

Los Feliz Mansion

If you were around L.A. around December of 1959, then you probably remember the gruesome murders that took place inside a Los Feliz mansion. On the night of December 6, Dr. Harold Perelson killed his wife with a hammer blow to the back of her skull. Then he tried the same act on his eldest daughter, but the blow was not as critical, and she managed to run away to get help. Her screams woke her little sisters, but Dr. Perelson assured them that it was only a dream and recommended that they go back to sleep. He then went on to take his own life by ingesting a deadly mixture of water, acid, and tranquilizer medication, leaving his three daughters parentless.[2] Although not much is known about their lives after that, we do know that the home was sold to a family who supposedly was not informed about the murder-suicide that had taken place just years before. Legends of a haunted house circulated quickly, and it is said that the new owners of the property fled on the anniversary of the deaths, leaving behind nearly all of their belongings.

Urban explorers reported seeing unwrapped gifts around an old Christmas tree for nearly fifty years while the house remained abandoned, frozen in time, and decaying. In 2016, it was finally bought and restored, only to then be abandoned again. It is uncertain what is going to happen to the home now, but there is a sign saying development, although nothing seems to have changed for several years now.

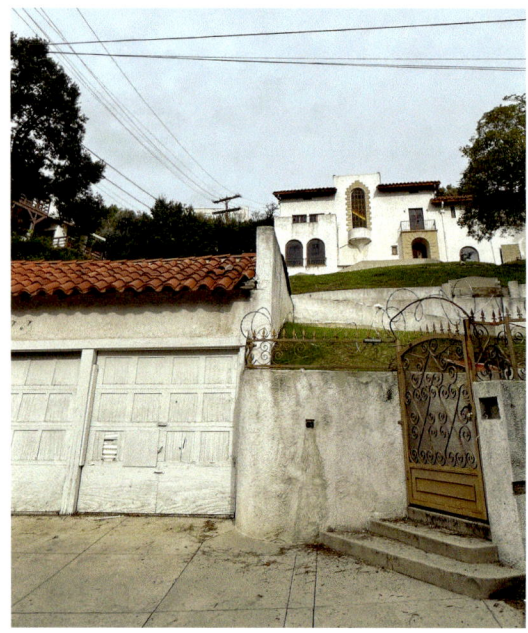

The front of the Los Feliz murder mansion. A broken home, shrouded in devastation, sits abandoned, surrounded by barbed-wire fences, for almost fifty years.

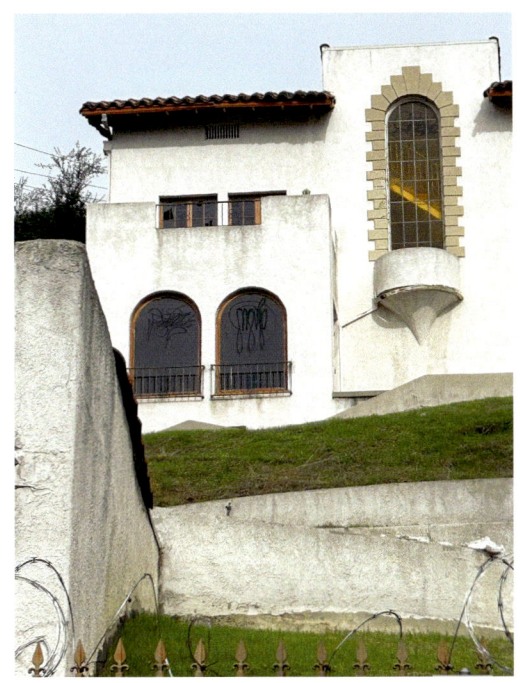 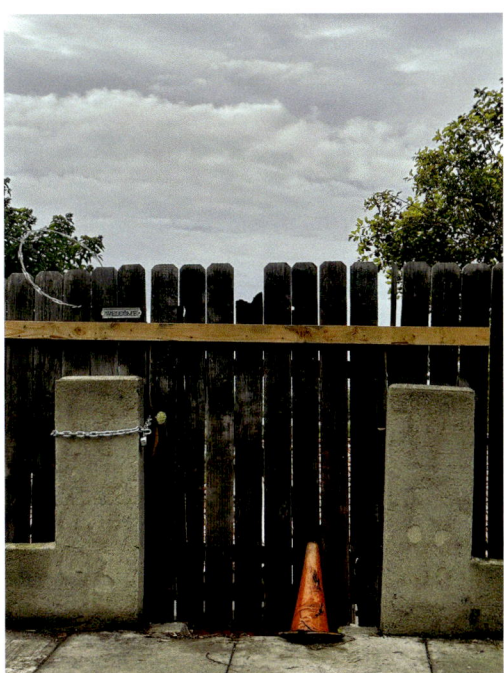

Above left: The graffiti-shattered windows and chipping paint do not make for the best selling point, but the home still holds much of its original beauty.

Above right: The Los Feliz murder mansion is sitting on over a half-acre, and the back gate exits to the street behind the house. The gate is boarded and chained up to prevent any vandalism, but it has been broken just enough for noisy snoopers to get a glimpse of the backyard.

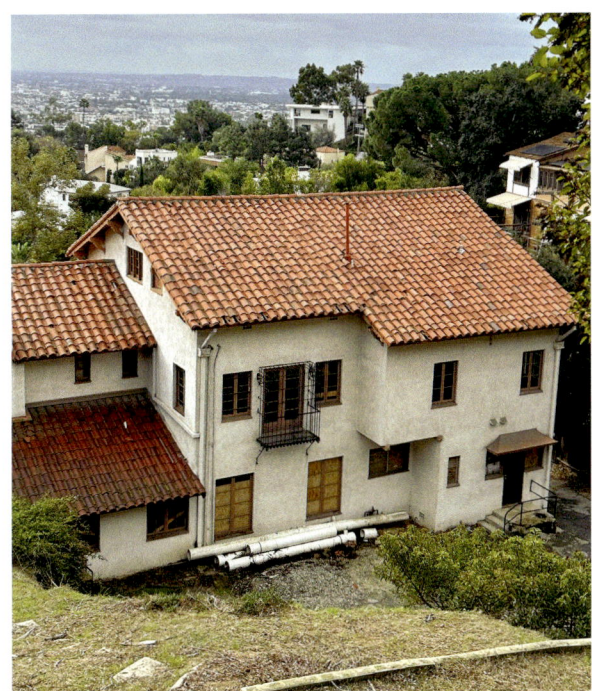

The view from the back of the murder mansion. What has the potential to be a very beautiful home with a large backyard just remains dark, overgrown, and boarded up.

Peacock House

This home was once worth over $4 million, but that price has dropped substantially since the home's state of neglect has increased. Sitting abandoned for over a decade, overgrown, and half burned, this home is destined for eventual demolition. The home sits on nearly 6 acres and was once known as the Peacock House because of several families of peacocks which decided to move in several years ago. Even the peacocks found it unsuitable, and now it has been reclaimed by homeless transients looking for quick shelter, and groups of teenagers looking for a place to party. Other residents in the area have been attempting to get the city to take action for years and have reported disturbances such as loud music, fires, and squatters. The property owner has attempted to redevelop the land into a multi-structure neighborhood, but it kept getting denied due to a protected species of live oak trees that inhabit the property. There are over fifteen protected trees that need to be relocated before any type of change can persist. So, until then, the land remains vacant.

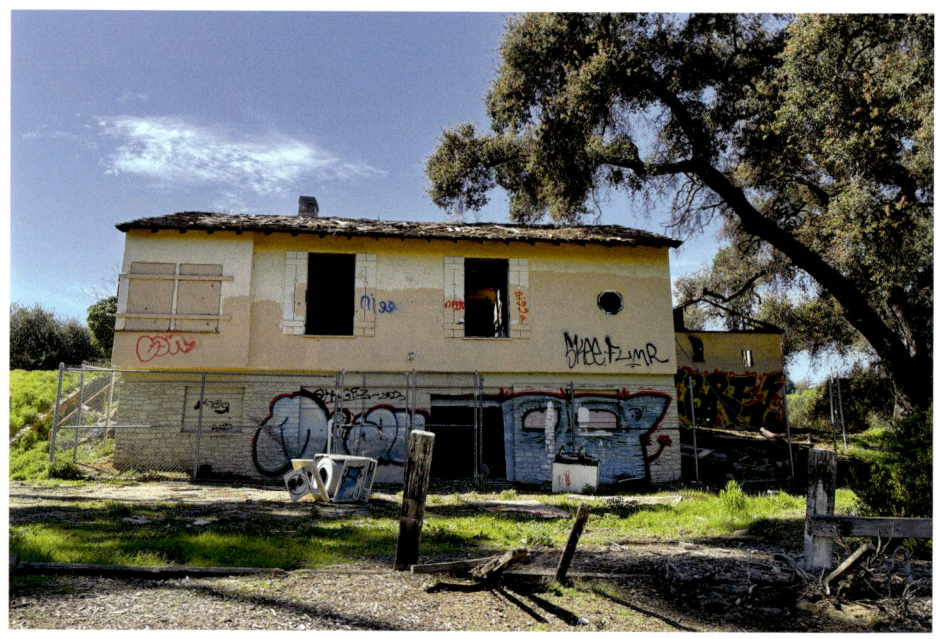

The front of the Mulholland Peacock House was once a beautiful estate, but it is now not much to look at.

Right: The homeowners boarded up all the windows and doors due to reports of squatters, but after a fire struck the property over a year ago, most of those boards were removed or burnt and now the entire home is surrounded by ivy and weeds.

Below: A fire that was likely set by a group of trespassers took out the back half of the home and severely damaged most of the interior.

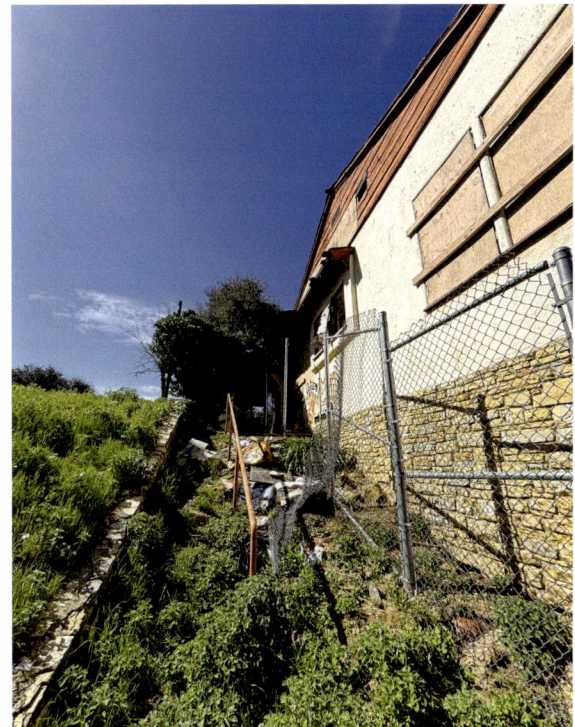

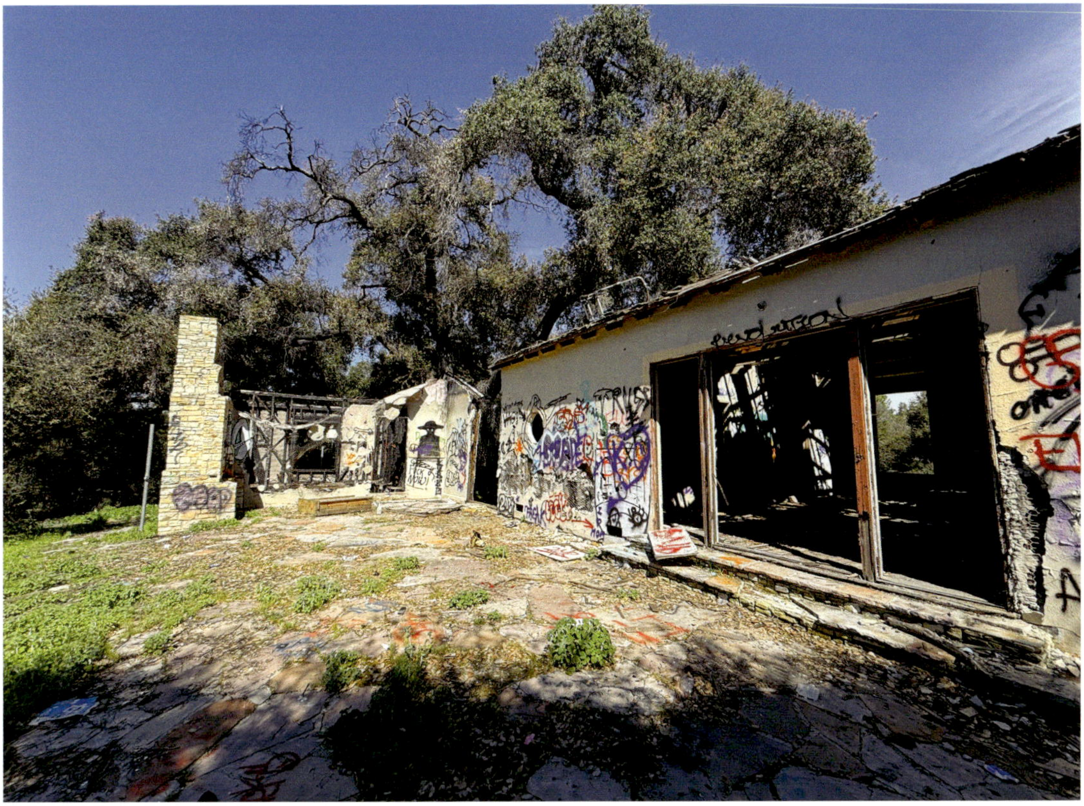

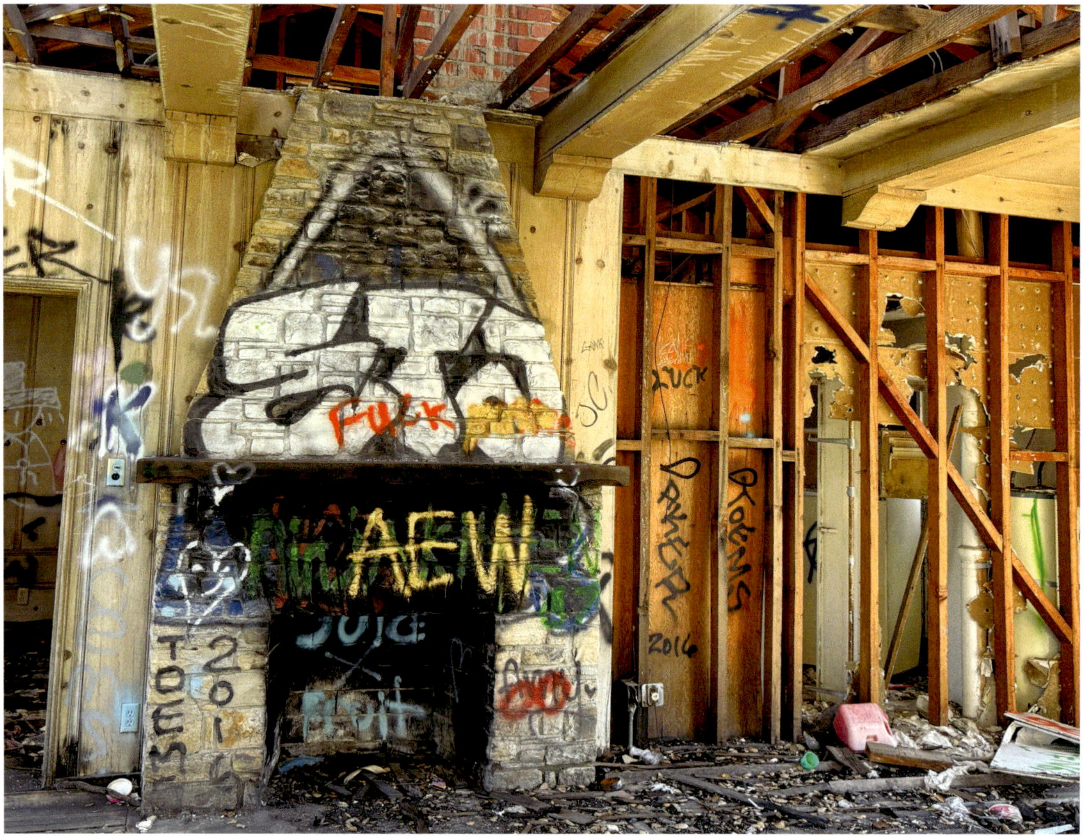

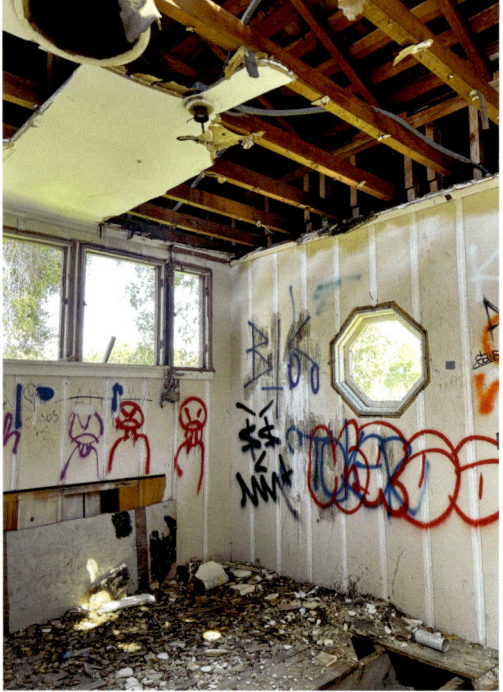

Above: A fireplace seems to be one of the renovations the home saw during its time. The bricks and stone of the main fireplace don't seem to line up, meaning this fireplace was likely remade just for looks and not for use.

Left: What does remain of the Peacock House is the skeleton of walls, a few wooden beams, unique windows, and two stone fireplaces.

Homeowner Troubles

Very few mansions in L.A. remain abandoned for more than a few years, but when faced with devastating damages and unsuitable insurance coverage, it can lead to major financial obligations that many homeowners cannot cover. Unfortunately, cases like this often leads to foreclosure, and unless an investor is willing to take on the challenges of the home's reconstruction, it often gets neglected for decades. After the pandemic, many families were faced with very hard times. Accidents happen, but during a fearful pandemic is one of the worst times for a disaster to occur. That is exactly what happened to the giant home and all the back duplexes behind it when a fire ripped through the area, leaving several families homeless. This property last sold in 2021 for $1.4 million, but as of now, no repairs have begun taking place.

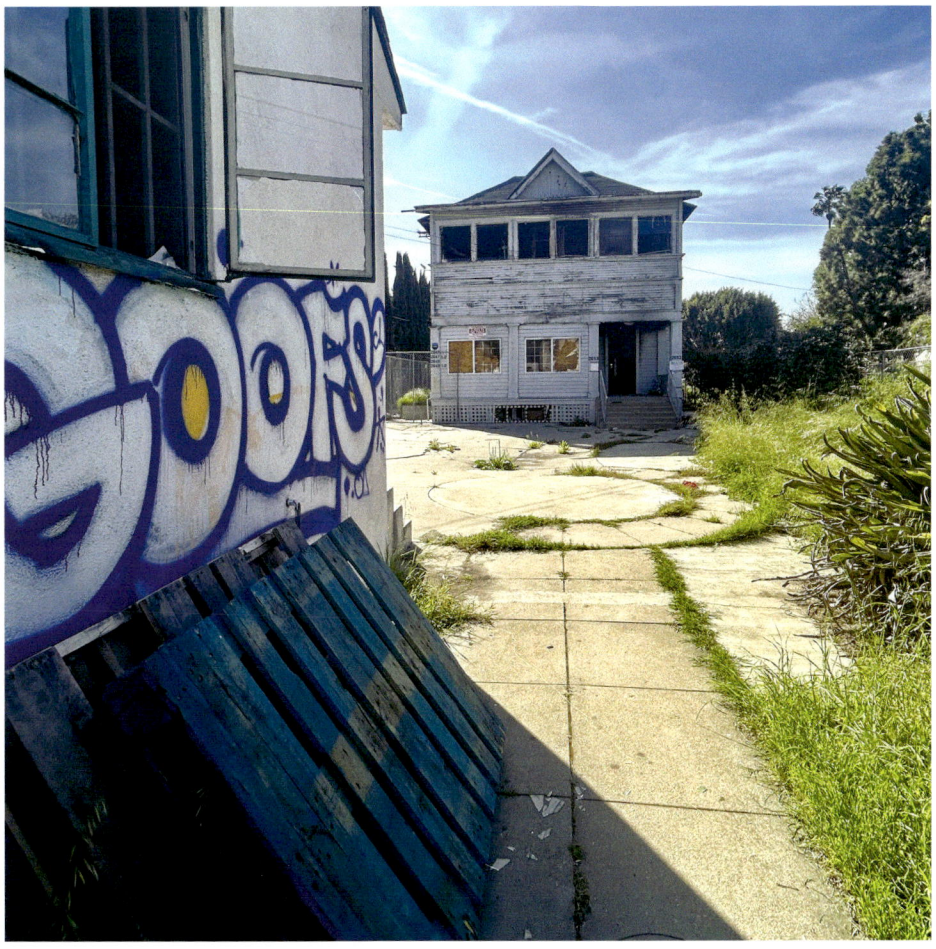

A devastating fire hit this home and the duplexes behind it, leaving many families homeless and this home without residence for going on three years now.

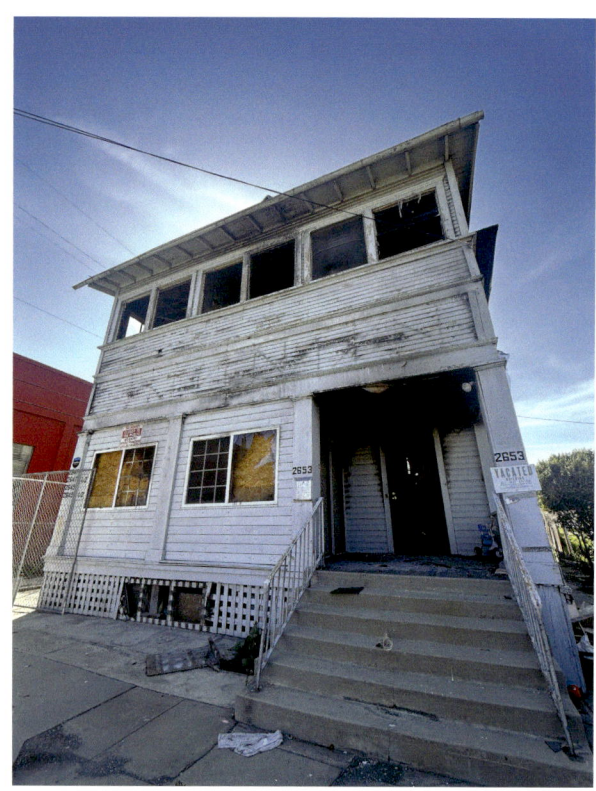

A large, multi-family home is now burnt to a crisp and looks like it will collapse at any moment.

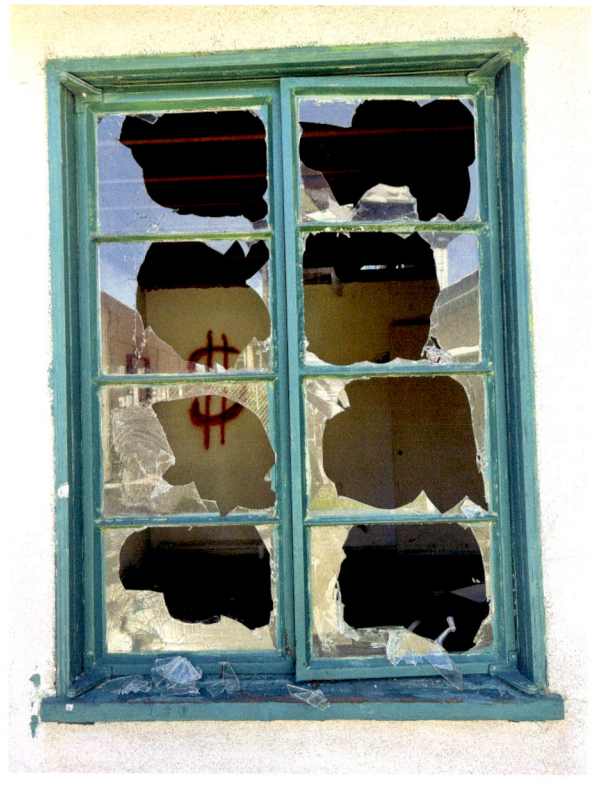

Vandals have come through and shattered just about every remaining window.

6

REMNANTS OF THE COLD WAR

The Cold War was an incredibly stressful time in America. With political and military tensions at an all-time high, the United States amped up its defense mechanisms to defend against a possible nuclear attack from the Soviet Union. In doing so, the military constructed over 200 Nike missile sites across the entire U.S., sixteen of which protected Los Angeles, known as the "Ring of Steel." It was equipped with anti-aircraft missiles called Nike-Ajax, then later followed by the Nike-Hercules, which were armed with nuclear warheads and could intercept incoming missiles.[1]

Site 88

L.A. missile site 88 sits perched on top of Oat Mountain in Chatsworth, supplying amazing views of the San Fernando Valley.

This site was considered active after its completion in 1953 and then decommissioned in 1974 but not demolished. It now sits open to the public, and is used often for police and F.B.I. training, yet it is falling apart and covered in graffiti. Although much of it has been removed, and what does remain is slowly crumbling, it is still one of the most intact missile sites in all Southern California and is an interesting place to see a piece of Los Angeles history.

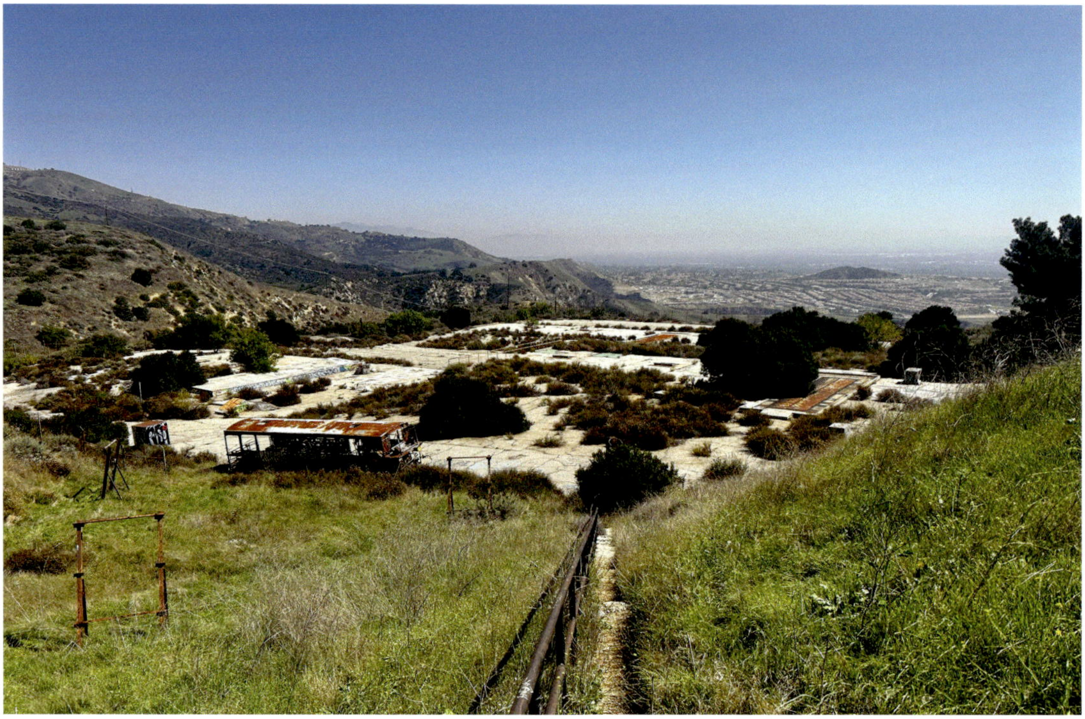

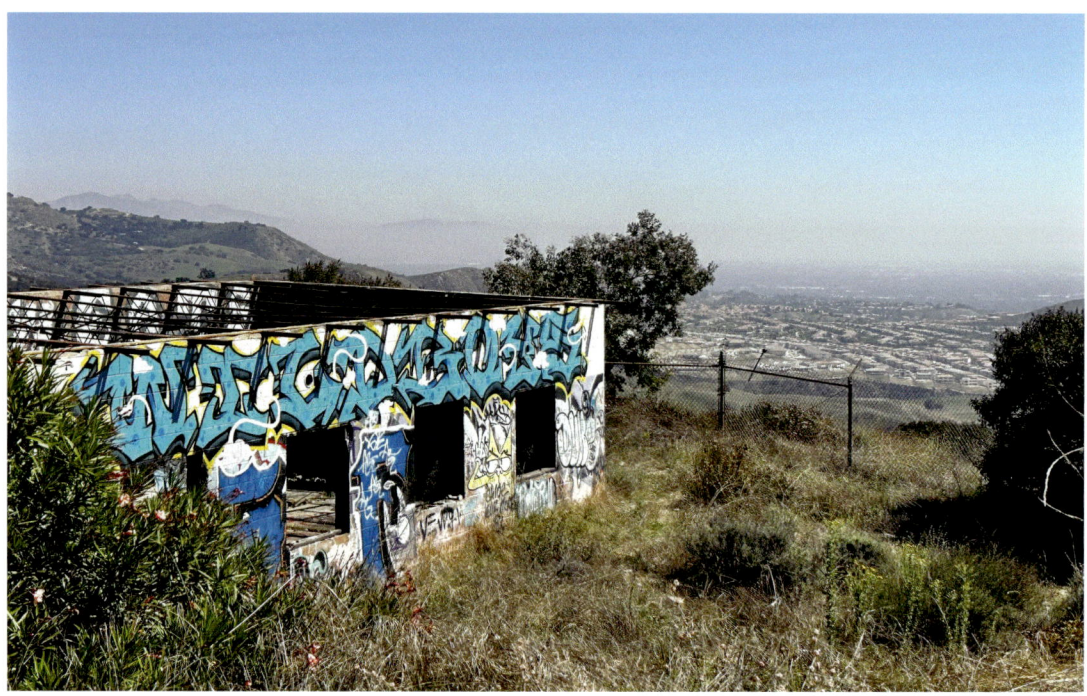

The view from the hill behind L.A. missile site #88. Over sixty years ago, this view would have consisted of multiple giant Nike-Ajax missiles, many of which were underground until testing or emergency use.

This missile site is one of the most intact of all sites in the area. Several structures, such as this one, remain, overlooking the San Fernando Valley.

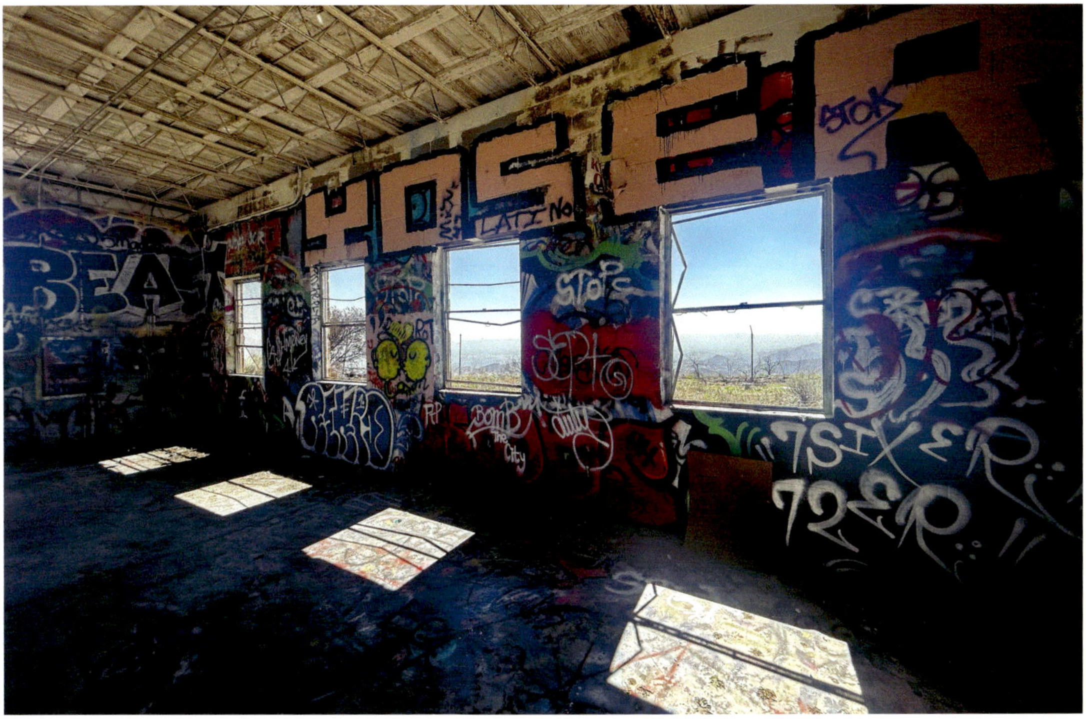

Most of the structures are now bullet-hole ridden, missing all the doors and windows, and only a few still have an intact roof.

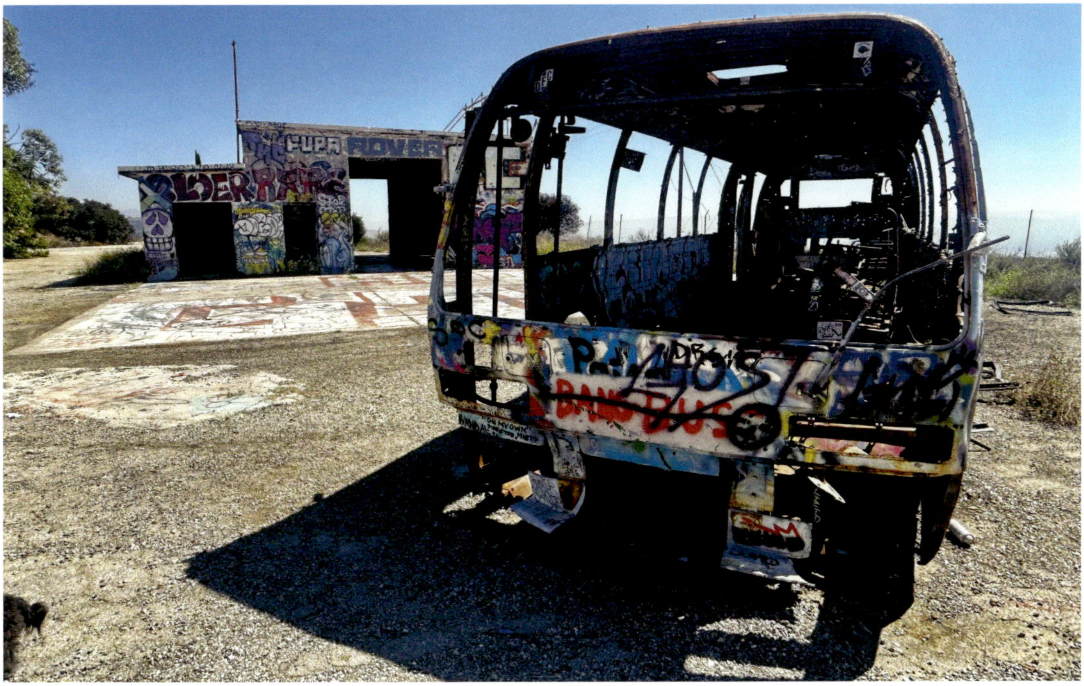

Since the missile site was decommissioned, it has been used for LAPD training exercises and target training.

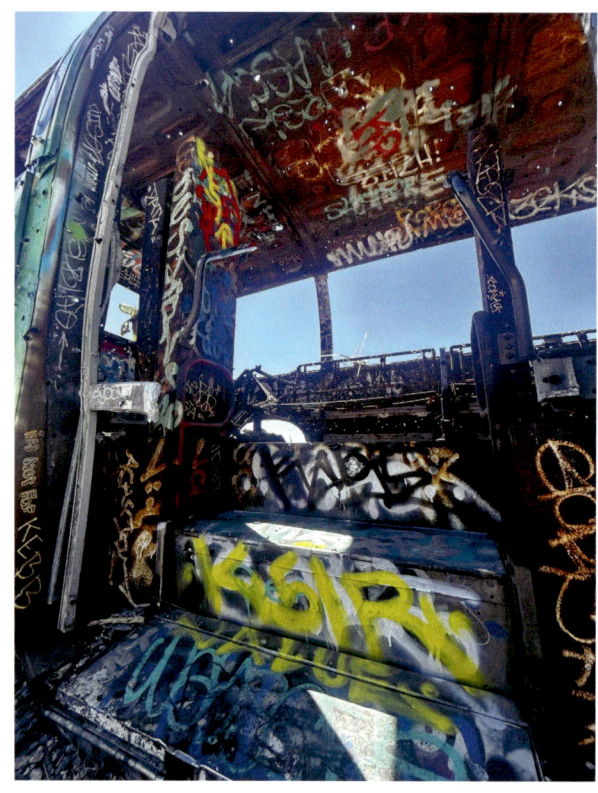

Several broken-down city buses were left on the old hilltop missile site and still play a role in the officer training courses.

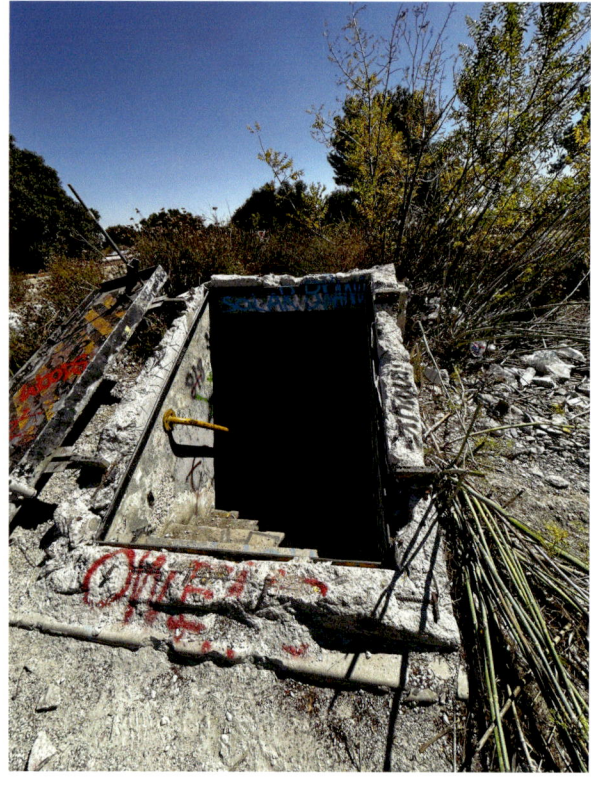

The launch site had several underground bunkers that were used to help operate the twelve different missiles on the site.

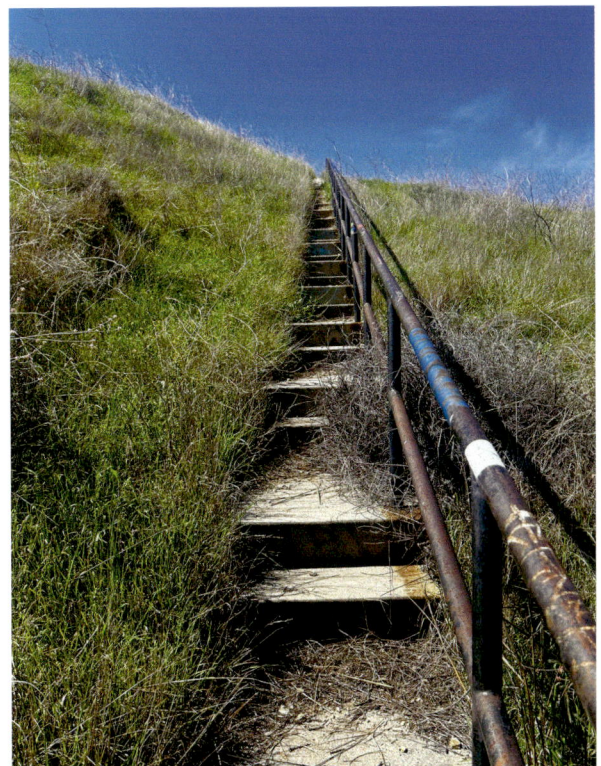

Right: These stairs once led to what was once the administration area but is now nothing but a large concentration of concrete slabs.

Below: Graffiti artists now use Nike missile site #88 as a large canvas for their different styles of street art. This artist used colors that complement the bright blue skies in Chatsworth.

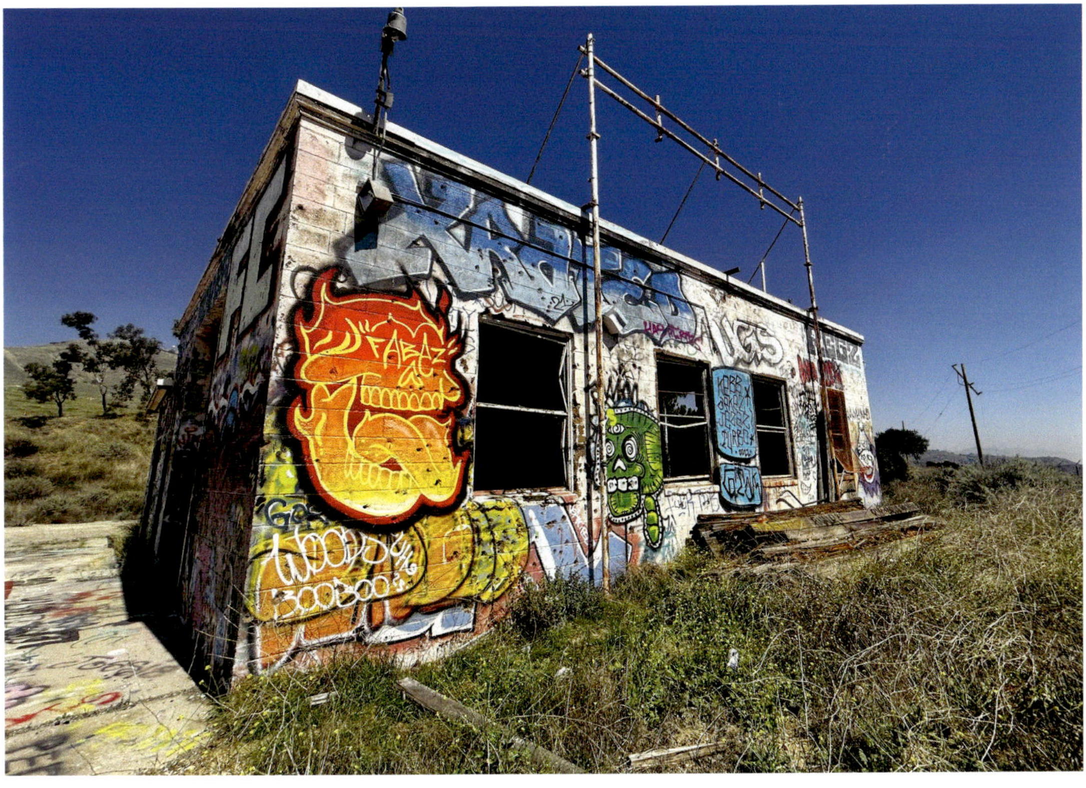

Control Site LA96C

Mulholland Hwy is an exceedingly popular road for commuters and beachgoers because it is one of the only roads that cuts across the mountains connecting the San Fernando Valley to the Pacific Coast. It also boasts beautiful views across almost the entire 30-mile stretch, but no view quite compares to the view from the top of the former Nike Missile Control Site LA96C. This site was a part of "The Ring of Fire," created to protect Los Angeles County from any possible missile strikes during the Cold War period. The army operated this site from 1956 to 1968, and during that time, missile control specialists were on guard 24/7 with the help of high-tech radar equipment to ensure no threats were headed to Los Angeles. Every missile site in Los Angeles starts with the name "Nike" because they were named after the Greek goddess of victory.[2] This site was decommissioned in 1968 and sat abandoned like the rest of the missile sites within the "Ring of Fire," and for many years, it was used as a party location for local teenagers. In 1996, the park was refurbished and became a public attraction where people could visit and appreciate its unique design and the beautiful 360 views from its observation deck. There are still many historical markers on this site explaining what was once taking place there.

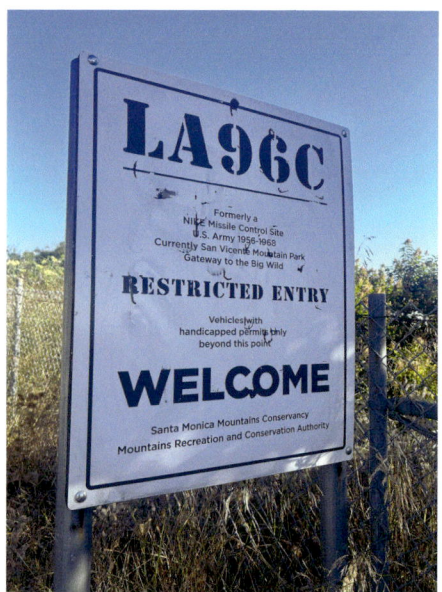 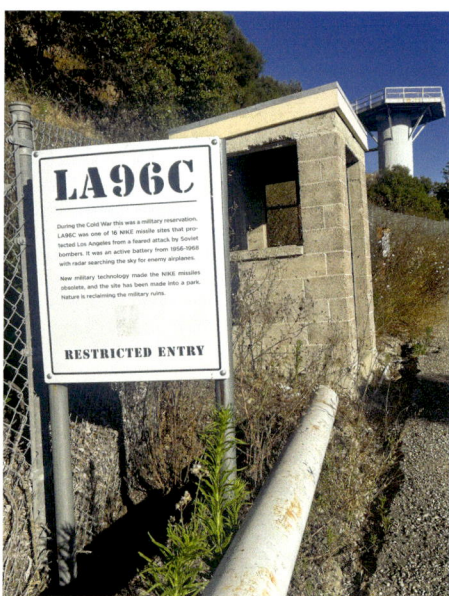

Above left: The sign at the driveway entrance to Nike missile control site LA96C displays a brief history of the site and explains that it is slowly being reclaimed by nature.

Above right: Another sign that was added to this missile base when it was first turned into a public park. These signs were provided in hopes that they would be used to provide information and history to all of its visitors.

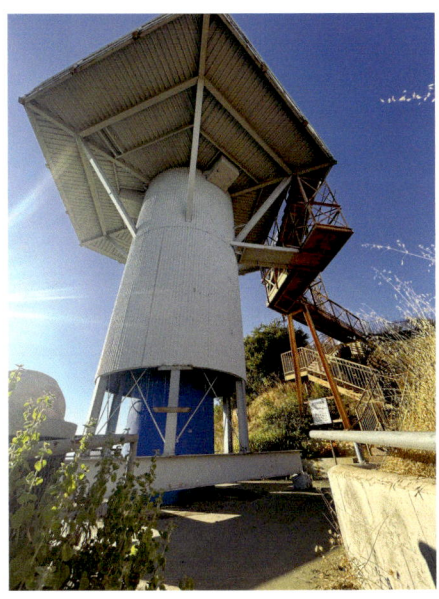 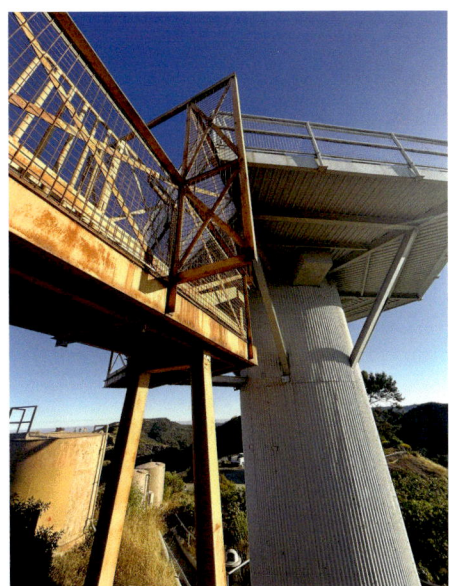

Above left: Standing underneath the observation tower and looking up, you can witness all of the rust and deterioration that this structure is starting to endure due to its changing environment and lack of upkeep.

Above right: The old, rusted site has been remodeled once to reintroduce it as a park; stairs and railings were added to make the deck easily accessible.

Below: The observation deck offers 360 views of the Santa Monica Mountains with a coin-operated telescope, and on a clear day you can see all the way to the Pacific Ocean.

Below right: These high-tech dishes and antennas were once used to help transmit signals across all the Nike missile bases throughout Southern California.

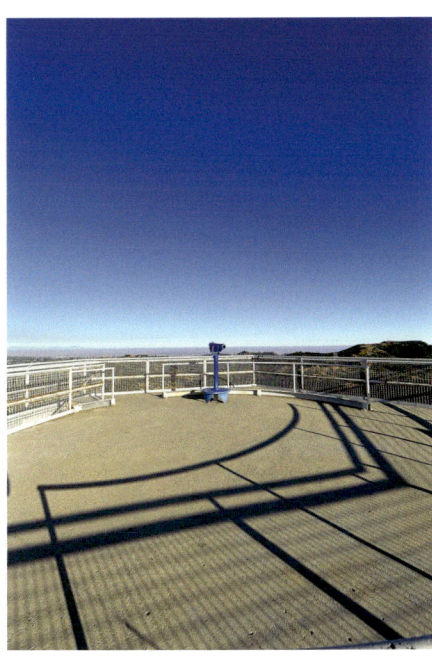 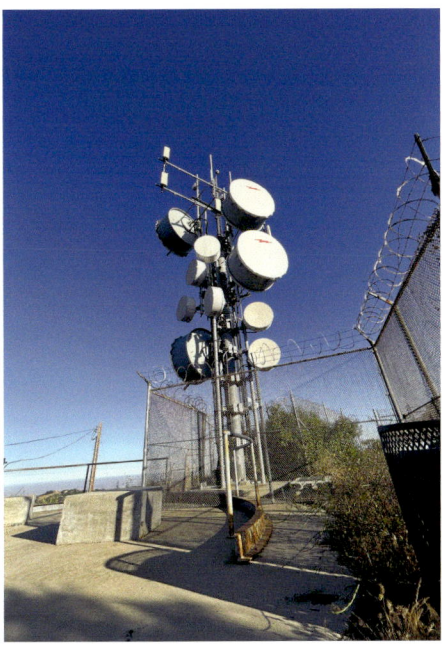

Battery Barlow-Saxton, Fort MacArthur

Another notorious site in San Pedro is Battery Barlow-Saxton at Fort MacArthur, sometimes referred to as Angel Gate Bunkers. Built in 1919, this site consisted of eight 12-inch M-1912 mortars mounted in batteries, which were used to protect the United States from attacks by sea. The guns could be rotated to protect all sides of the quarry and could shoot up to 11 miles. This battery also consisted of underground bunkers that I am not able to find much information on and which have been closed off for decades. By 1943, all the guns had been retired, all the entrances to the bunkers were welded shut, and Battery Barlow-Saxton was officially abandoned.[3] All that is left is the historic cement quarry, which is secured by two large fences and a patrol officer. Despite the risk, it has become a canvas for graffiti artists, and a playground for many risky urban explorers.

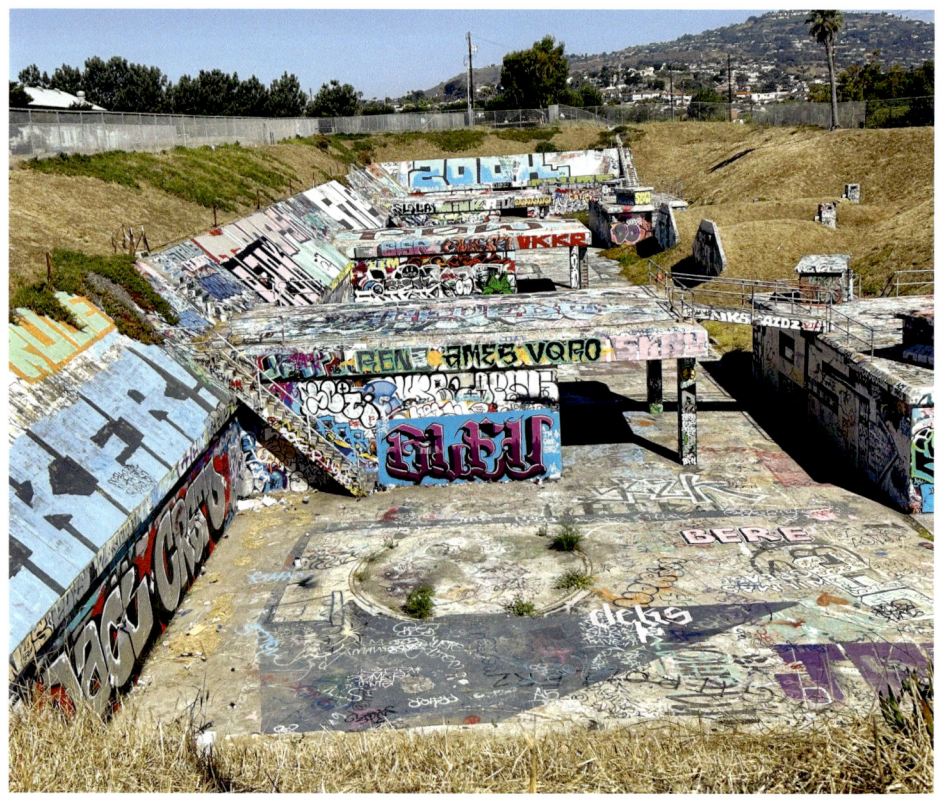

A bird's-eye view looking through one of the chain-link fences protecting the notorious Battery Barlow-Saxton at Fort Macarthur from trespassers.

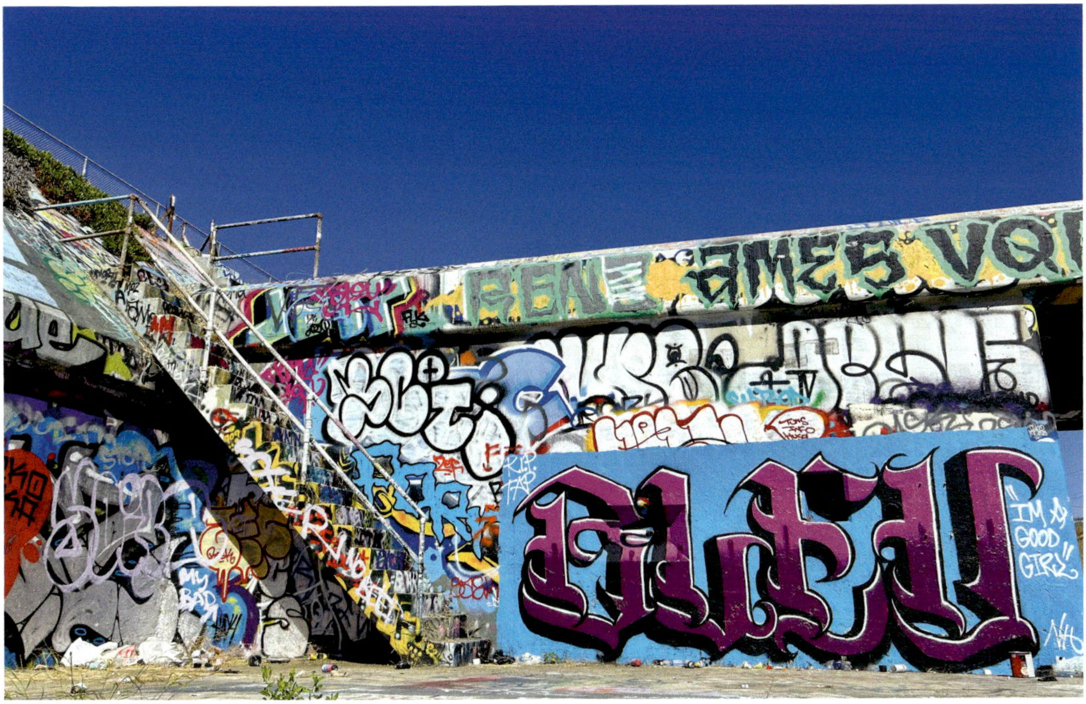

Above: The site is dug into a hill about 50 feet deep and reinforced with giant concrete walls, with steps on each corner to ensure easy escape in case of possible evacuations.

Right: Most of the site has now been covered in graffiti and is not maintained, although a security guard does patrol the area and will kick out trespassers if found.

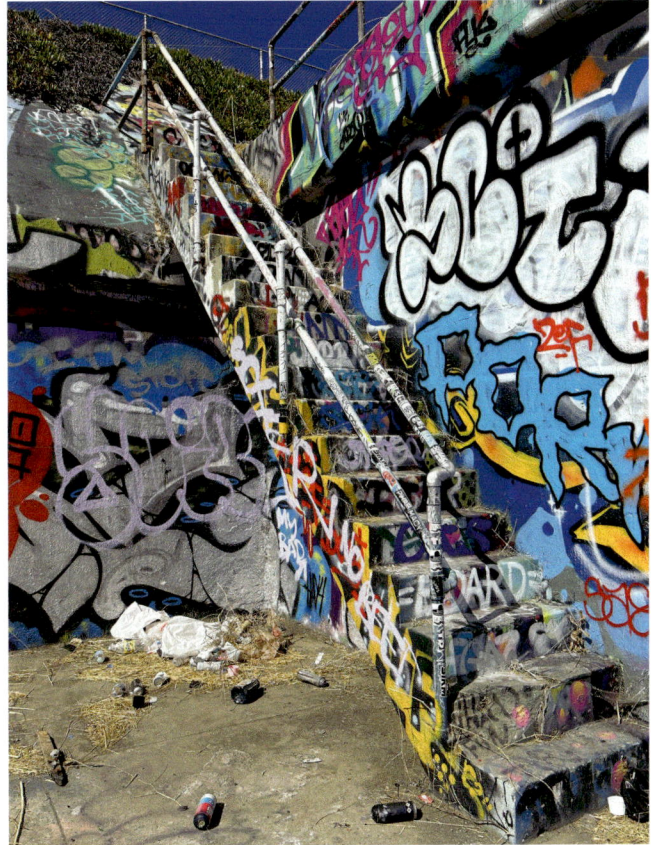

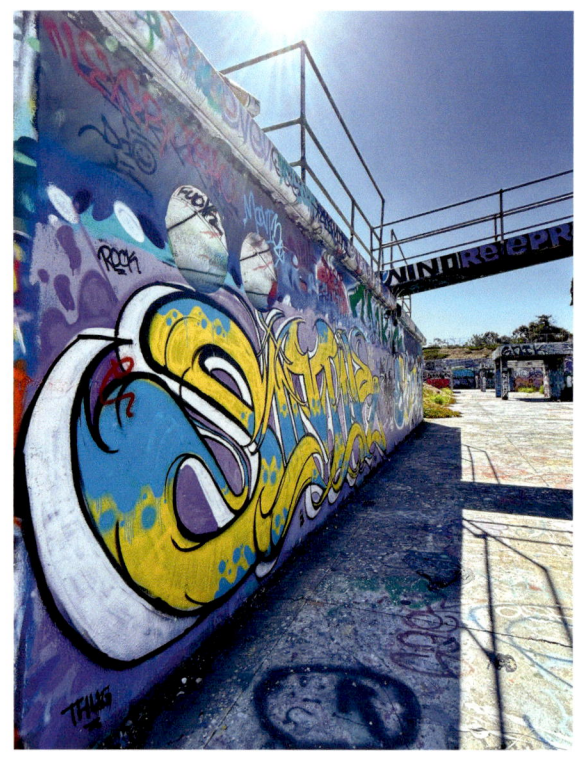

A lot of the graffiti is done using bright, vibrant colors, and it creates a perfect opportunity for photographers to capture some great shots of the cement bunkers and narrow pathways.

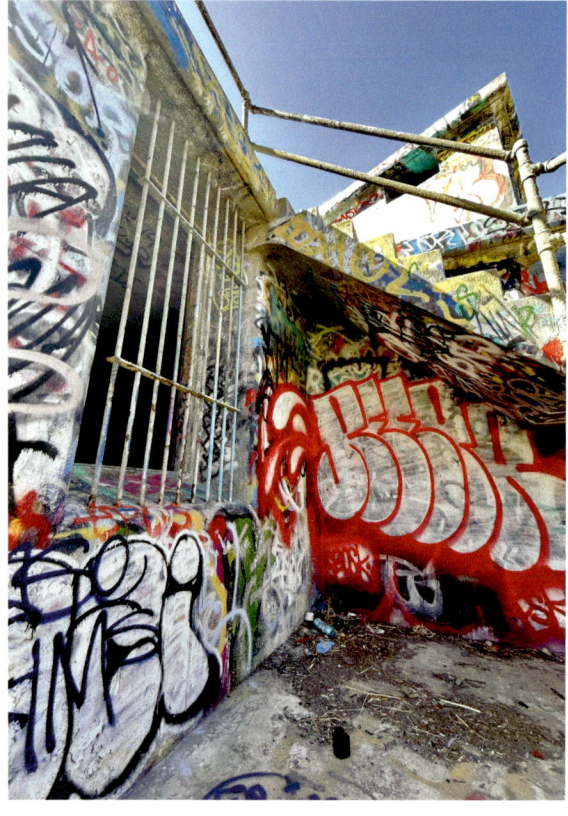

Battery Barlow-Saxton has underground bunkers that were used mainly as control sites for the batteries but would also play a role in protecting the soldiers during missile launches, although they have all been welded shut now to prevent trespassing.

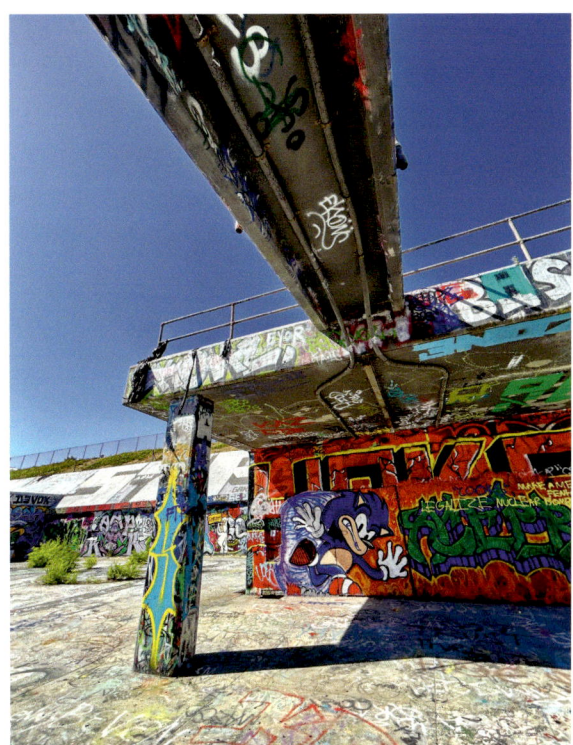

Right: The site had pathways on top of the structures so that the operators could reach all the operating parts of the launching equipment.

Below: What was once a notorious battery site is now a giant cement canvas for the brave trespassers and street artists to express themselves.

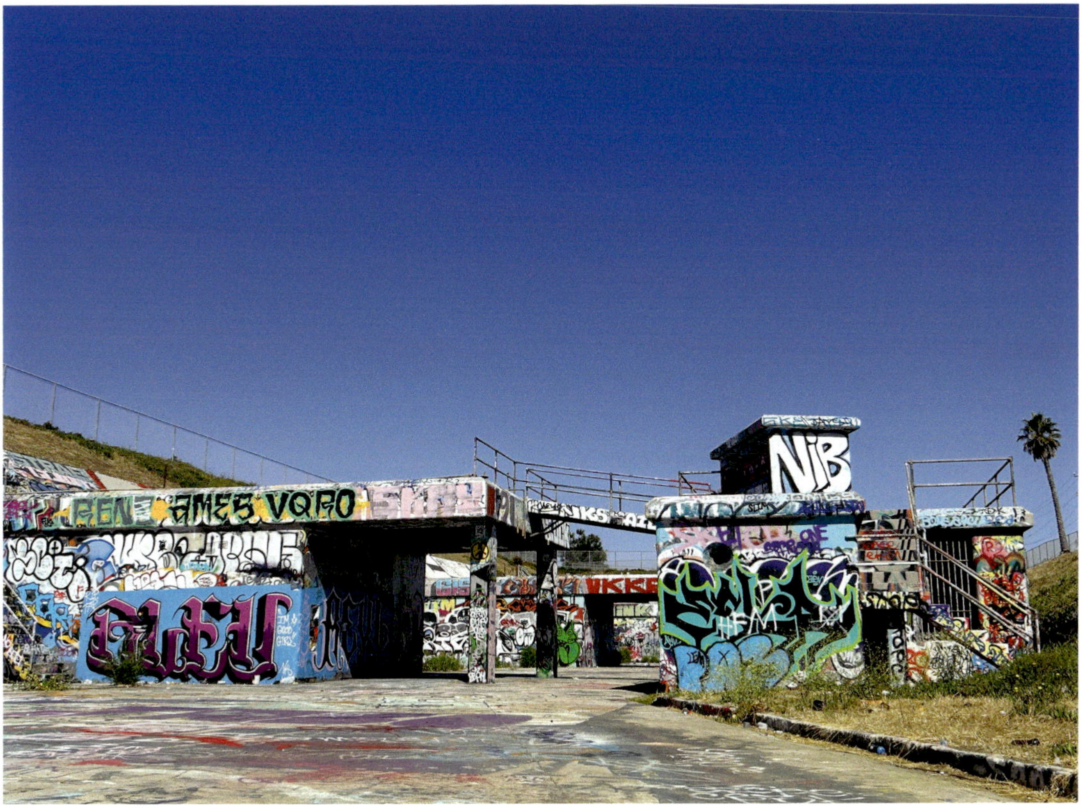

EPILOGUE
THE END IS NEVER CERTAIN

When people see abandoned buildings, they often think that they are a terrible eyesore or a nuisance, but rarely consider the rich history, nor realize how beautiful the location once was. Therefore, places often get neglected, until being forcibly demolished, but every now and then, these places are left alone and slowly get reclaimed by nature until there is nothing left but rubble. I find it so interesting to investigate these lost places, and during my explorations, I have found that with the right angles and lighting, you can capture beauty in pretty much anything, even in a pile of rubble. Every structure has its story, whether the story is full of laughter and joy or heartache and tears. Although some of the stories are dark, mysterious, and creepy, they still play a role in this county's history, and they deserve to be remembered. Some are lucky enough to be restored and preserved while others remain, dilapidated and crumbling, either way, they are beautiful recollections of the past.

Through photography and lots of research, I am happy to have shared with you some of these unique locations that helped form the county of Los Angeles into what it is today. From the city to the mountains, deserts, and beaches, this area is scattered with abandoned gems waiting to be discovered. I hope you enjoyed the journey, and if you are interested in seeing these places firsthand, all I ask is that you be careful and respectful. Many of these locations can be extremely dangerous, or even illegal to enter, so please use caution and common sense. Urban exploration is a fun reminder that it is not always about what is on the outside, and that when you dive a little deeper, you may discover something truly unbelievable.

ENDNOTES

Chapter 1

1   friendsofgriffithpark.org/griffith-park-zoo-the-great-world-zoo-that-never-was-1912-1966/.
2   www.laconservancy.org/learn/historic-places/barlow-respiratory-hospital/.
3   www.laconservancy.org/learn/historic-places/lincoln-heights-jail/#:~:text=Built%20in%20
    1927%20at%20a,hold%20up%20to%202%2C800%20prisoners.
4   atomicredhead.com/2020/02/25/the-ghostly-remnants-of-the-old-la-county-poor-farm/.
5   www.loc.gov/item/ca3514/#:~:text=The%20County%20Poor%20Farm%20began,Los%20
    Angeles%20County%20Hospital%20system.
6   memory.loc.gov/master/pnp/habshaer/ca/ca3500/ca3509/data/ca3509data.pdf.
7   www.californiacuriosities.com/sunken-city/.

Chapter 2

1   la.curbed.com/2014/9/24/10043624/murphy-ranch-trail-pacific-palisades-history.
2   www.undeavors.com/post/solstice-canyon-spectacular-views-a-bit-of-history-and-a-
    peaceful-waterfall.
3   www.atlasobscura.com/places/canned-heat-suicide-house#:~:text=But%20urban%20
    legend%20gives%20us,By%20dawn%2C%20he%20was%20dead.

Chapter 3

1   valleyrelicsmuseum.org/general-museum-news/mentryville-remnants-of-valley-
    history/#:~:text=On%20September%2026%2C%201876%2C%20Charles,the%20
    area%20effectively%20named%20Mentryville.
2   californiathroughmylens.com/big-horn-mine-vincent-cabin/.

Chapter 4

1   scvhistory.com/scvhistory/lw3095.htm.

Chapter 5

1   www.latimes.com/local/lanow/la-me-ln-boyle-heights-peabody-werden-20160630-snap-story.html.
2   historythings.com/haunting-story-los-feliz-murder-mansion/.

Chapter 6

1   www.chatsworthhistory.com/Program%20Downloads/Nike%20Missile%20Base%20History%20-%20LA88%20Chatsworth.pdf.
2   www.hmdb.org/m.asp?m=146037.
3   barlow-saxton.htm.